I0621822

# The Gospel of Jesus

# &

# The Sure Mercies Of David

## A Story of Grace & Mercy

Clifford Brant Beaver

The Gospel of Jesus & The Sure Mercies of David
A Story of Grace & Mercy

ISBN: 979-8-9903038-0-5
ISBN: 979-8-9903038-1-2
ISBN: 979-8-9903038-2-9

All Scripture references are from the King James Version Bible

*The Holy Bible, King James Version*. Cambridge Edition: 1769; *King James Bible Online*, 2024. www.kingjamesbibleonline.org.

Some scripture is underlined and/or emboldened. This is done to emphasize certain words or phrases although it is not in the original text.

This Book is Dedicated to Valerie, Isabel, and Carter

# Table of Contents

## The Gospel of Jesus

## The Sure Mercies of David

## Part 1
## The Gospel of Jesus

The Gospel of Jesus is about what the Gospel is and what it is not. There's nothing more important than understanding and believing the Gospel of Jesus. This is more important than who you marry, what job you have, where you live, your physical health, your financial wellbeing, and anything else that you think is important. What you do with the Gospel of Jesus determines where you'll spend Eternity. There are many false gospels that claim to be true. A false gospel cannot save you. The only way to know if you're believing the True Gospel is to verify it through the Bible. The purpose of this Book is to show you what the True Gospel is.

# The Ministry of John the Baptist

All stories have a beginning. For Israel, the beginning of the Messiah's revealing started with John the Baptist. Granted, Jesus had already been born, with wonders testifying of the miraculous birth, not to mention all the prophesies that were given by the Old Testament Prophets.

However, the birth of Christ was a somewhat private matter, and only a chosen few were aware of who Jesus was until after His Baptism, and after His ministry began. There had been a quiet time in Israel, with no major Prophet or King to act as an intercessor between the common man and God. They were being oppressed by the Romans and were seeking a deliverer. Most of the Priest and Religious Leaders had traded true fellowship with God for a Dead Religion, which appeared strict and holy outwardly but had no true power or relationship with God. It was at this time, and in this environment, when John the Baptist came on the scene. The Old Testament Prophets Isaiah and Malachi had both prophesied of John and had told that one would come who would go before The Lord, and prepare His way, or prepare the hearts of the people to receive Him.

| Isaiah 40:3 The voice of him that crieth in the wilderness, **Prepare ye the way of the LORD**, make straight in the desert a highway for our God. | Malachi 3:1 Behold, I will send my messenger, and **he shall prepare the way before me**: and **the LORD**, whom ye seek, shall suddenly come to his temple, **even the messenger of the covenant**, whom ye delight in: behold, he shall come, saith the LORD of hosts. |
|---|---|

John's ministry was in the wilderness (in the country outside of town) and he began preaching and telling the people that they needed to Repent because the Kingdom of Heaven was about to arrive on earth (Repent ye, for the Kingdom of Heaven is at hand). This is the Kingdom that was prophesied to Israel in the Old Testament. They were told that a King (The Messiah) would come who would set up a Kingdom on Earth and would rule with His Saints forever.

| Daniel 2:44 And in the days of these kings **shall the God of heaven set up a kingdom, which shall never be destroyed**: and the kingdom shall not be left to other people, but it shall break in pieces and consume all these kingdoms, and it shall stand for ever. | Daniel 7:27 And the kingdom and dominion, and the greatness of **the kingdom under the whole heaven**, shall be given to the people of the saints of the most High, whose kingdom is an everlasting kingdom, and all dominions shall serve and obey him. |
|---|---|

The reason John could say the Kingdom was at hand or arriving is because the King of the Kingdom was about to arrive and make Himself known to the people.

To have a Kingdom you must first have a King. You see, a Kingdom is made up of a King, the King's subjects or servants who are under his rule, and a piece of geography. The Kingdom has not yet come into its fullness. The Kingdom of Heaven was rejected by the leadership of Israel when they rejected Jesus as King. We are living now in a time of postponement similar to what Israel experienced in the wilderness when they feared to enter the promised land (this was all in God's plan so that Gentiles and all the Church could be part of the Kingdom). The Kingdom of Heaven will find its fulfillment when Christ returns at the second coming and reigns as King over all the world with His saints.

Matthew 23:13 But woe unto you, scribes and Pharisees, hypocrites! for **ye shut up the kingdom of heaven against men**: for ye neither go in yourselves, neither suffer ye them that are entering to go in.

It's important at this point that you understand what the word Repent means. The word Repent has become confused and misinterpreted, with many people thinking it strictly means to stop sinning or to change your mind about sin. This is incorrect. The word Repent as it's used in the Bible, means "To Change or To Turn", and the context will define what one is to turn from and to what one is to turn to. It could refer to a Change of Mind or it could refer to a physical change or turn of direction. God repents several times in the Bible and most of the time when He repents, He is turning from one course of action to another. It's usually in the context of Him stopping His chastisement on His people and showing them mercy after they repent…

Psalm 106:44 Nevertheless he regarded their affliction, when he heard their cry:
Psalm 106:45 And **he remembered for them his covenant, and repented** according to the multitude of his mercies.

So, what did John tell the people to turn from and to what were they to turn to? They were to repent of trusting in their own righteousness and to admit they were sinners, and to trust that the Messiah who was coming was going to save them from their sins. They were to stop believing that their good works could save them, and to trust fully in what the Messiah was going to do as a means for their salvation.

Let's look at John's mission one more time which is recorded in Luke Chapter 1. John is told here that he is going to be the Lord's prophet who will give an understanding to the people that the Lord was coming to take away their sins, and this will be accomplished when the Lord visits us and shows us Mercy. It's important here to notice that salvation and the removal of sins will come when God visits us and shows us Mercy.

Luke 1:76 And thou, child, shalt be called the prophet of the Highest: for thou shalt go before the face of the Lord to prepare his ways;
Luke 1:77 **To give knowledge of salvation unto his people by the remission of their sins,**
Luke 1:78 **Through the tender mercy of our God**; whereby the dayspring from on high hath visited us,

Furthermore, see some of John's own words in John 3 (Spoken by John the Baptist).

> John 3:30 He must increase, but I must decrease.
> John 3:36 **He that believeth on the Son hath everlasting life**: and he that believeth not the Son shall not see life; but the wrath of God abideth on him.

The Apostle Paul also explains John's message to a group of disciples in Acts 19 and explains how that John's message of Repentance was to believe upon the one to come after him who was Jesus.

> Acts 19:4 Then said Paul, John verily baptized with the baptism of repentance, **saying unto the people**, that they should believe on him which should come after him, that is, on Christ Jesus.

Now, in order to be baptized by John the people were required to confess that they were sinners in need of salvation. The act of water baptism itself pictures the death of the person and their burial, and then them being raised and brought back to life by God. You see, a living person doesn't need to be brought back to life because they are alive. However, if you realize that you are dead in your sins then you can see your need for a new life. Dead people can't change their ways in order to become alive again, because they are dead! The only way a dead person can come back to life is if God gives them a new life and a new birth (you must be born again).

Most of the common people of Judaea had recognized John as a prophet and thereby had received his message. The Pharisees also acknowledged John as a righteous man and as a prophet, and some had tried to be baptized by him themselves however, they were denied because of their self-righteousness.

Matthew 3:5 Then went out to him Jerusalem, and all Judaea, and all the region round about Jordan,
Matthew 3:6 **And were baptized of him in Jordan, confessing their sins**.
Matthew 3:7 But when he saw many of the Pharisees and Sadducees come to his baptism, he said unto them, O generation of vipers, who hath warned you to flee from the wrath to come?
Matthew 3:8 **Bring forth therefore fruits meet for repentance**:
Matthew 3:9 And think not to say within yourselves, We have Abraham to our father: for I say unto you, that God is able of these stones to raise up children unto Abraham

Luke goes on to tell us in Chapter 7 how that most of the common people accepted John's message, but the Pharisees and lawyers rejected the notion that they were sinners who needed to be saved in the same way that a publican or harlot needed salvation.

Luke 7:29 And all the people that heard him, and the publicans, **justified God, being baptized with the baptism of John**.

Luke 7:30 **But the Pharisees and lawyers rejected the counsel of God against themselves**, being not baptized of him.

In Matthew 21, Jesus has one of His last conversations with the Pharisees. He explains to them how the harlots and publicans will be in God's Kingdom, but that they would not. The harlots and publicans had understood their sinful condition, but even after seeing the change that had taken place in those people's lives, the pharisees still refused to believe the message.

> Matthew 21:31 Whether of them twain did the will of his father? They say unto him, The first. Jesus saith unto them, Verily I say unto you, That **the publicans and the harlots go into the kingdom of God before you**.
> Matthew 21:32 For John came unto you in the way of righteousness, and ye believed him not: **but the publicans and the harlots believed him: and ye, when ye had seen it, repented not afterward, that ye might believe him.**

At another time Jesus spoke to some people and He confronted a theology that was prevalent in that day as well as in the day we live. Most people believe that it's the bad people who will be punished, and who will go to hell, like murders, adulterers, thieves, etc. The people of Jesus's day believed this also, and they also believed that these Galilaeans who had suffered this punishment must have been worse sinners than themselves and that God only punished really bad sins. The truth is all sinners will be punished and perish eternally unless those sinners repent of their current belief system and put their trust and their hope of salvation in Christ and what He accomplished.

> Luke 13:1 There were present at that season some that told him of the Galilaeans, whose blood Pilate had mingled with their sacrifices.
>
> Luke 13:2 And Jesus answering said unto them, **Suppose ye that these Galilaeans were sinners above all the Galilaeans, because they suffered such things?**
>
> Luke 13:3 **I tell you, Nay: but, except ye repent, ye shall all likewise perish.**

We'll visit repentance a little further later. Ultimately John died for his faith and for making a stand for righteousness. However, he accomplished the purpose and the plan that God had for him. He introduced Israel to their Messiah and had prepared their hearts to receive the Word that Jesus was about to give them.

# Christ the Son of God

Nearly everyone in the world has heard of the name Jesus Christ. The World commonly uses this name as a curse word. Most of the time people do this in ignorance without knowing they are committing blasphemy, while others do it intentionally to mock God.

The word Christ is not actually the last name of Jesus although that is how it is often used. Christ is not a last name at all but rather it is a Title. The word Christ is another name for Messiah, and it means "The Anointed One".

| John 1:41 He first findeth his own brother Simon, and saith unto him, We have found the **Messias, which is, being interpreted, the Christ.** | John 4:25 The woman saith unto him, **I know that Messias cometh, which is called Christ**: when he is come, he will tell us all things. |
|---|---|

The Old Testament Prophets had prophesied of a coming Messiah. The prophet Daniel had prophesied about when the Messiah would arrive in Israel and when He would be cut off or killed.

Daniel 9:25 Know therefore and understand, that from the going forth of the commandment to restore and to build Jerusalem **unto the Messiah the Prince shall be seven weeks, and threescore and two weeks**: the street shall be built again, and the wall, even in troublous times.
Daniel 9:26 **And after threescore and two weeks shall Messiah be cut off,** but not for himself: and the people of the prince that shall come shall destroy the city and the sanctuary; and the end thereof shall be with a flood, and unto the end of the war desolations are determined.

To fully understand who Jesus Christ is, it's important for you to understand how the Bible defines Christ. Christ is not just another human being. Christ is special and separate from all other human beings who ever walked the earth. In fact, Christ or, The Messiah, is God in human form! Isaiah prophesies of the Spirit speaking to John the Baptist (the voice of one crying in the wilderness). The Spirit tells John what he is to say and to proclaim to Israel. John is to prepare the way of the Lord that is coming, and in verses 9 and 10, the Spirit says to proclaim that the Lord that is coming is God.

Isaiah 40:9 O Zion, that bringest good tidings, get thee up into the high mountain; O Jerusalem, that bringest good tidings, lift up thy voice with strength; lift it up, be not afraid; say unto the cities of Judah, **Behold your God!** Isaiah 40:10 **Behold, the Lord GOD** will come with strong hand, and his arm shall rule for him: behold, his reward is with him, and his work before him.

Speaking of the coming Messiah, in Chapter 9 Isaiah also shows us that the child who would be born and given to Israel would be called the Mighty God.

Isaiah 9:6 For **unto us a child is born, unto us a son is given:** and the government shall be upon his shoulder: and **his name shall be called** Wonderful, Counsellor, **The mighty God**, The everlasting Father, The Prince of Peace.

The Prophet Micah tells us that the Messiah, the ruler that's coming to Israel is eternal.

Micah 5:2 But thou, Bethlehem Ephratah, though thou be little among the thousands of Judah, yet out of thee shall **he come forth unto me that is to be ruler in Israel; whose goings forth have been from of old, from everlasting.**

Jeremiah prophesies of the Branch from David (David's descendant) who will be King. The Name of the King will be Jehovah Tsidkenu or as the King James Bible translates, The Lord Our Righteousness.

Jeremiah 23:5 Behold, the days come, saith the LORD, that **I will raise unto David a righteous Branch, and a King shall reign and prosper**, and shall execute judgment and justice in the earth.
Jeremiah 23:6 In his days Judah shall be saved, and Israel shall dwell safely: and this is **his name whereby he shall be called, THE LORD OUR RIGHTEOUSNESS.**

The Old Testament speaks of the Holy One in many places. Isaiah tells us that the Holy One would be despised and hated by the nation of Israel.

> Isaiah 49:7 Thus saith the LORD, the Redeemer of Israel, and **his Holy One, to him whom man despiseth, to him whom the nation abhorreth**, to a servant of rulers, Kings shall see and arise, princes also shall worship, because of the LORD that is faithful, and the Holy One of Israel, and he shall choose thee.

Isaiah also tells us in Chapter 47 that the Holy One is our Redeemer.

> Isaiah 47:4 As for **our redeemer**, the LORD of hosts is his name, **the Holy One of Israel**.

The Holy One is also our King.

> Psalm 89:18 For the LORD is our defence; and **the Holy One of Israel is our king.**

Habakkuk shows us that the Holy One is God.

> Habakkuk 1:12 **Art thou not from everlasting, O LORD my God, mine Holy One?** we shall not die. O LORD, thou hast ordained them for judgment; and, O mighty God, thou hast established them for correction.
> Habakkuk 3:3 **God came from Teman, and the Holy One** from mount Paran. Selah. His glory covered the heavens, and the earth was full of his praise.

In Psalm 16, we see a prophecy of the Holy One dying but not seeing corruption, meaning His body would not decay.

> Psalm 16:10 For thou wilt not leave my soul in hell; **neither wilt thou suffer thine Holy One to see corruption.**

Peter preaching in Acts, tells the people that Christ is the Holy One and that Jesus is the Christ.

Acts 2:27 Because thou wilt not leave my soul in hell, neither wilt thou suffer thine **Holy One** to see corruption.

Acts 2:31 He seeing this before **spake of the resurrection of Christ**, that his soul was not left in hell, neither his flesh did see corruption.

Acts 2:32 **This Jesus hath God raised up**, whereof we all are witnesses.

Christ the Son of God is God in human form. The Son was seen in the Old Testament. Anytime a person has seen an image of God they were seeing the Son of God. God is triune meaning three in one (Father, Son & Holy Spirit). God the Father is like the Soul of God. The Father has no image, and no one has ever seen Him for He is Spirit.

| John 1:18 **No man hath seen God at any time**, the only begotten Son, which is in the bosom of the Father, he hath declared him. | John 6:46 **Not that any man hath seen the Father, save he which is of God**, he hath seen the Father. |
|---|---|

The three Hebrew Children who were thrown into the fiery furnace had an encounter with the Son of God.

Daniel 3:25 He answered and said, Lo, I see four men loose, walking in the midst of the fire, and they have no hurt; and **the form of the fourth is like the Son of God.**

Isaiah saw the God of Israel. He saw The Lord on His throne and in His temple, and he saw the seraphim giving Him praise.

> Isaiah 6:1 In the year that king Uzziah died **I saw also the Lord sitting upon a throne, high and lifted up, and his train filled the temple.**
>
> Isaiah 6:2 Above it stood the seraphims: each one had six wings; with twain he covered his face, and with twain he covered his feet, and with twain he did fly.
>
> Isaiah 6:3 And one cried unto another, and said, **Holy, holy, holy, is the Lord of hosts: the whole earth is full of his glory.**

Isaiah speaks to the Lord and the Lord gives him a message about the people of Israel.

> Isaiah 6:10 Make the heart of this people fat, and make their ears heavy, and shut their eyes; lest they see with their eyes, and hear with their ears, and understand with their heart, and convert, and be healed.

John tells us in Chapter 12 of his Gospel that the Lord who Isaiah saw was Jesus!

> John 12:40 He hath blinded their eyes, and hardened their heart; that they should not see with their eyes, nor understand with their heart, and be converted, and I should heal them.
>
> John 12:41 **These things said Esaias, when he saw his glory, and spake of him.**

Now, Christ the Son of God is the express image of God. I used to think of the Father as an Old Man and the Son as we typically think of Jesus, a younger version of God. This is not the case. The Father is not an Old Man and Jesus as a young man as we envision Him, is not His glorified form. Remember the Father has no image, He is invisible. The Son is the image of the invisible God and the express image of the person of God.

| Colossians 1:15 **Who is the image of the invisible God,** the firstborn of every creature: | Hebrews 1:3 **Who being the brightness of his glory, and the express image of his person,** and upholding all things by the word of his power, when he had by himself purged our sins, sat down on the right hand of the Majesty on high: |
|---|---|

The Son also created all things in Heaven and Earth.

| Colossians 1:16 **For by him were all things created, that are in heaven, and that are in earth,** visible and invisible, whether they be thrones, or dominions, or principalities, or powers: all things were created by him, and for him: | Hebrews 1:2 Hath in these last days spoken unto us **by his Son,** whom he hath appointed heir of all things, **by whom also he made the worlds** |
|---|---|

Another name for the Son of God is the Word. God speaks through His Word and it's another way of stating that the Son reveals God to us.

> John 1:1 **In the beginning was the Word, and the Word was with God, and the Word was God.**
>
> John 1:2 The same was in the beginning with God.
>
> John 1:3 **All things were made by him; and without him was not any thing made that was made.**

When I was growing up, I thought that the Father was so glorious that it would kill you to look at Him, but the Son while also glorious, was of a lesser glory so that we could see Him. I thought this because of the verses in Exodus where Moses wants to see God's glory and God tells Moses that if he sees His face, it will kill him. You see, I knew that people were able to look at Jesus, and so naturally I thought this was the Father and that He was of a different nature than the Son. However, I didn't understand the nature of the glory of God. You see, Moses didn't understand what he was asking for when he wanted to see God's glory.

> Exodus 33:18 And he said, I beseech thee, **shew me thy glory.**

Remember, the Son created all things. Let me ask you something, what is more glorious, the sun in our solar system or the Son of God who created the sun? The Son of God is of course more glorious. The Sun is approximately 93-94 million miles from us on Earth and yet if we looked at the sun in all its glory on a bright day it would damage our eyes. If we were next to the sun, we would be instantly incinerated.

Do you really think you could look at the Son of God in all His glory and live? In 1 Timothy, Paul states that Jesus Christ dwells in light that no man can approach. Does that sound familiar to Exodus and Moses?

> 1 Timothy 6:14 That thou keep this commandment without spot, unrebukable, until the appearing of **our Lord Jesus Christ**:
> 1 Timothy 6:15 Which in his times he shall shew, who is the blessed and only Potentate, the King of kings, and Lord of lords;
> 1 Timothy 6:16 Who only hath immortality, **dwelling in the light which no man can approach unto**; **whom no man hath seen, nor can see**: to whom be honour and power everlasting. Amen.

It's important to understand that God is not bound by space and time in the same way we are. You see, God is outside of space and time. That means God can be in different places at the same time. As a man Jesus was limited to His physical body, but as the Glorified Son of God He is not. So, if God wants the Son of Man to stand next to the Son of God, that is not an issue. That's important to understand because in the Bible we read about the Son of Man coming to the Ancient of Days in Daniel and then in Acts, Stephen sees Jesus standing by God.

The Son of Man is Jesus in human form. Being the Son of Man means Jesus came from a man. Being the Son of God means Jesus came from God. Jesus was both man and God at the same time! He was fully man at the same time being fully God. However, Jesus in His human form, was not His true form. He humbled Himself and took on flesh as a man.

> Philippians 2:5 Let this mind be in you, which was also in Christ Jesus:
> Philippians 2:6 **Who, being in the form of God, thought it not robbery to be equal with God**: [7] But made himself of no reputation, and **took upon him the form of a servant, and was made in the likeness of men:**

When he says, thought it not robbery to be equal with God, he is saying that God didn't think it would be robbing, or taking away anything from His nature or holiness to become a human being.

When Moses met the Lord at the burning bush, he asked God what name he should call Him and God told Moses to call Him "I AM". Jesus takes on the identity of "I AM" in the Gospels.

| Exodus 3:14 And God said unto Moses, I AM THAT I AM: and he said, Thus shalt **thou say unto the children of Israel, I AM hath sent me unto you.** | John 8:58 Jesus said unto them, Verily, verily, I say unto you, **Before Abraham was, I am.** John 8:59 **Then took they up stones to cast at him**: but Jesus hid himself, and went out of the temple, going through the midst of them, and so passed by. |
|---|---|

The reason the Jews wanted to stone Jesus is because they understood what He was saying. When Jesus said, "I am" He was saying He was the I AM who spoke to Moses. In the Gospel of John, there are 7 "I AM" statements of Jesus.

I Am the Bread of Life – John 6:35

I Am the Light of the World – John 8:12

I Am the Door – John 10:7

I Am the Good Shepard – John 10:11

I Am the Resurrection and the Life – John 11:25

I Am the Way the Truth and the Life – John 14:6

I Am the True Vine – John 15:1


You may wonder why it's so important that you understand who Christ is. This is important because God is clear throughout the Bible that God alone is Savior and Creator. If Jesus isn't God, He can't be your Savior.

Isaiah 43:11 I, even I, **am the LORD; and beside me there is no saviour.**

Jesus is our Lord, the Holy One, the Creator of Israel, and our King.

Isaiah 43:15 **I am the LORD, your Holy One**, the creator of Israel, your King.

We wait for the appearing of Jesus Christ who is our God and Savior.

Titus 2:13 Looking for that blessed hope, and the glorious appearing of **the great God and our Saviour Jesus Christ;**

God is a Trinity. I can't explain God's nature, nor can I fully understand it as a man, because God is so far beyond us and our understanding. I can only describe what God reveals to us in His word. The best way I personally make sense of the Trinity is by thinking of the Trinity in Three in the same way we are three, as in Body, Soul, and Spirit. I think of the Father as the Soul of God, the mind, will, emotions, the decision-making center. The Son is the Body, and the Holy Spirit is God's Spirit, the ultimate essence of His nature of Love, Justice, Etc. God unlike humans can separate Himself into three persons and He can have conversations with Himself; the Father speaks to the Son, the Holy Ghost makes intercession to the Father on the Saints behalf, etc. However, at the same time the Bible tells us that all fulness of the Godhead dwells bodily in the Son.

> Colossians 2:9 For in him dwelleth all the fulness of the Godhead bodily.

This means when you have the Son, the Holy Spirit is there, and when you see the Son, you see the Father also. Jesus told the Apostles that they had seen the Father. This confused Phillip a little and so Phillip asked the Lord to show him the Father. Jesus then told Phillip that by seeing Him, he had seen the Father.

> John 14:7 If ye had known me, ye should have known my Father also: and **from henceforth ye know him, and have seen him**.
> John 14:8 Philip saith unto him, Lord, **show us the Father**, and it sufficeth us.
> John 14:9 Jesus saith unto him, Have I been so long time with you, and yet hast thou not known me, Philip? **he that hath seen me hath seen the Father;** and how sayest thou then, Show us the Father?

The Godhead bears witness in Heaven that Jesus is Christ the Son of God and these Three are One. The Word is another name for the Son.

> 1 John 5:7 For there are three that bear record in heaven, the Father, the Word, and the Holy Ghost: **and these three are one**.

It's hard to wrap your mind around the Trinity, impossible actually. To understand that Jesus is God in Flesh, it must be revealed to you from the Father.

> Matthew 16:15 He saith unto them, But **whom say ye that I am**?
>
> Matthew 16:16 And Simon Peter answered and said, **Thou art the Christ, the Son of the living God.**
>
> Matthew 16:17 And Jesus answered and said unto him, Blessed art thou, Simon Barjona: **for flesh and blood hath not revealed it unto thee, but my Father which is in heaven.**

If anyone tells you that Jesus is not God in Flesh, they are either ignorant or of the spirit of Antichrist. Very few people deny that Jesus of Nazareth walked the earth, but nearly everyone except a true Christian will deny that Jesus is God in Flesh. When the New Testament writers write of Jesus Christ, remember Christ is not the last name of Jesus. What they are saying is Jesus the Messiah, or Jesus the Christ, or simply put Jesus Christ.

> 2 John:7 For many deceivers are entered into the world, **who confess not that Jesus Christ is come in the flesh. This is a deceiver and an antichrist.**

Christ is the Son of God. He is God in Human form. God was manifested in the flesh, which means He was shown and revealed to us in a body of flesh.

> 1 Timothy 3:16 And without controversy great is the mystery of godliness: **God was manifest in the flesh**, justified in the Spirit, seen of angels, preached unto the Gentiles, believed on in the world, received up into glory.

The Apostles realized that Jesus is God. Remember, God says that He alone is Lord, and He alone is Savior. In order for Jesus to be your Savior, He must also be your God.

> John 20:28 And Thomas answered and said unto him, **My LORD and my God.**

To Thomas, Jesus is his Lord and his God. Is Jesus your Lord and your God?

# The Gospel of Jesus Christ

What do you think of when you hear the word, Gospel? A popular phrase among Christians is "that's the gospel truth" which is meant to convey that something said is exceptionally true. The Gospel is exceptionally true but what exactly is it? If you were tasked with conveying the Gospel to someone, would you know how? The first thing to come to your mind may be one of the four books in the Bible known as the Gospels- Matthew, Mark, Luke, and John. While the Gospel message is contained within each of these books, the entire books themselves are not "The Gospel". If you met someone on the street who had just been in an accident and had minutes to live, you wouldn't try to read one of the four Gospels to them in order that they might have a chance to believe and be saved. Rather, what you should do is convey to them the Gospel of Salvation message which is contained within each of these books as well as within all the books of the New Testament. Of course, to do that you would need to understand the Gospel yourself. Now the word Gospel itself simply means <u>a message of good news or good tidings</u>.

| Isaiah 52:7 How beautiful upon the mountains are the feet of him that bringeth **good tidings, that publisheth peace**; that bringeth **good tidings of good**, that publisheth salvation; that saith unto Zion, Thy God reigneth! | Romans 10:15 And how shall they preach, except they be sent? **as it is written**, How beautiful are the feet of them that preach **the gospel of peace**, and bring **glad tidings of good things**! |
|---|---|

(Paul quoting Isaiah, notice good tidings & gospel are interchangeable)

Something that I was confused about for a while is the fact that the disciples were sent out to preach the Gospel early in Jesus's ministry (Matthew 10, Luke 9-10), and yet days or weeks before the crucifixion when Jesus tells the disciples He's going to the cross, they reject His message, and you have the famous verses where Jesus talking to Peter says "Get Behind Me Satan" (Matthew 16, Mark 8). So, what's going on here? Were the disciples preaching a Gospel that they themselves did not understand or receive? The answer is, they were preaching a different Gospel.

First, let me go ahead and establish something, there is only One Gospel of Salvation, which is the Gospel of Jesus Christ. However, there were other messages of good news that were proclaimed. There was the Gospel of the Kingdom of Heaven, which was a message of good news that God was going to set up a physical Kingdom on this earth which He would reign over. John the Baptist proclaimed this message and that the Messiah who was Jesus, was about to arrive. After John was arrested, Jesus began preaching the Gospel of the Kingdom of God.

| Mark 1:14 Now after that John was put in prison, Jesus came into Galilee, preaching the gospel of the kingdom of God, |
|---|

The Gospel of the Kingdom of God was a message of good news about how there was going to be a reconciliation between mankind and God, which would come through faith in the Messiah. This Gospel would later merge with the Gospel of Jesus Christ; the only difference is that when Jesus first began preaching about the Gospel of the Kingdom it was not fully understood by the people as to how it would be accomplished. When the disciples were sent out in Matthew 10, they preached the Gospel of the Kingdom and were telling the people that the Messiah-Jesus had arrived and was bringing God's Kingdom. After Jesus rose from the dead, they understood the full story about how this would be accomplished. This brings us to the Gospel of Jesus Christ, aka the Gospel of Salvation, which is a message of good news that tells us what Jesus did for us, to save us, and to restore us to God.

Before we take a closer look at this Gospel, let's examine first why we need it. When a person is sick, they'll take medication to get better even if the medicine doesn't taste good, or they'll get stuck with a needle even if they fear it being painful. However, normally they would only do this if they're first convinced that they have a sickness and that the medicine they are taking will make them better. This Gospel will save your soul if you accept it, but you must receive and accept it. You see, I have bad news for you. You have an incurable and fatal sickness. Your soul is infected with Sin. Sin is a transgression of God's law, and every human being that's ever walked this earth save One has had its infection. If you've sinned one time, you're a Sinner.

| 1 Kings 8:46 If they sin against thee, (**for there is no man that sinneth not**,) and thou be angry with them, and deliver them to the enemy, so that they carry them away captives unto the land of the enemy, far or near; | Ecclesiastes 7:20 For **there is not a just man upon earth, that doeth good, and sinneth not.** | Psalm 14:3 They are all gone aside, they are all together become filthy: **there is none that doeth good, no, not one.**<br><br>Romans 3:23 **For all have sinned, and come short of the glory of God**; |
|---|---|---|

You may say okay, but what's the big problem since everyone sins? The problem is that Sin separates you from God. All who sin die. Your body and your soul will die. Death is a separation. Physical death separates your spirit from your body. Spiritual Death separates your soul from God. This spiritual death needs to be your biggest concern because if it isn't corrected, you'll be separated from God in Hell and eternally in the Lake of Fire.

Because of God's holiness, He won't be in the presence of anything that is sinful. Then you ask, how many sins does it take to kill me? It takes one sin in your entire lifetime. It started with one sin in the Garden of Eden. God gave Adam one rule to follow and told him if he disobeyed, he would die. Religion's lie is that if you can straighten up and be a little better than the rest, don't sin too much, just every now and then, and no really awful sins, then God can forgive and accept you. That's a Lie. God is Holy and Righteous, and He will not be in the presence of any sin whatsoever, not one white lie, not one covetous thought, not one moment of pride. If you sin once, you're dead.

| Genesis 2:17 But of the tree of the knowledge of good and evil, thou shalt not eat of it: for in the day that thou eatest thereof **thou shalt surely die.** | Ezekial 18:4 Behold, all souls are mine; as the soul of the father, so also the soul of the son is mine: **the soul that sinneth, it shall die.** |
|---|---|

Okay, so can you see that we have a huge problem? You say then, since we've already sinned what hope do we have? Well, God did something Amazing! God is Love and He didn't want you to die. God figured out a way to give you a new life, a way to separate your soul from your sins. He came up with this plan before He made the world! He would become a human being and live a perfect life. God the Son would come into the world and follow all the laws of God the Father. God became a man and put on flesh. He humbled Himself for us and took upon Himself a body of flesh and blood.

He did everything right and never sinned, not once. Furthermore, He would suffer the wrath of God for every sinner. He would take on Himself all our sins and suffer and die and would experience separation from the Father. In doing so, He could satisfy God's Justice (all that sin must die). The writer of Hebrews makes the point that in the Old Testament, anytime God remitted sins something had to shed its blood and die. This was a shadow of what God was going to do in the future. It took the shedding of the blood of Christ to remove our sins.

Hebrews 9:22 And almost all things are by the law purged with blood; and **without shedding of blood is no remission.**

When He did this, He recovered what Adam lost. Jesus Christ became the Perfect man and the Head (Leader) of all those who would accept Him. Now, when God the Father looks at those who are under the Headship of Christ, He doesn't see us as sinners but as perfect Children of God! God can forgive us and pardon our sins while at the same time remaining Just, because all the wrath we deserved was laid upon Jesus. His Word is preserved because Jesus took our place and died our death for us. God now associates us with our Perfect Righteous Leader, and because of Christ, we can once again have a relationship with God!

Now, the Gospel of Jesus Christ is presented all throughout the New Testament but there is one place where it is presented the most clearly so that it cannot be argued against. This is in 1 Corinthians Chapter 15. In this chapter, Paul declares the Gospel of Salvation that he preached to the Corinthians. Notice, he says this is what they received, what they stand in, and is what they are saved by, so long as they keep it in memory and don't move away from it.

---

1 Corinthians 15:1 Moreover, brethren, **I declare unto you the gospel which I preached unto you**, which also ye have received, and wherein ye stand;

1 Corinthians 15:2 **By which also ye are saved**, if ye keep in memory what I preached unto you, unless ye have believed in vain.

1 Corinthians 15:3 For I delivered unto you first of all that which I also received, **how that Christ died for our sins according to the scriptures;**
1 Corinthians 15:4 **And that he was buried, and that he rose again the third day according to the scriptures:**

---

Jesus died for our sins because our sins demanded death. If we could clean up our lives and become righteous ourselves, Jesus would not have needed to die. Because He was sinless, death had no power to hold him (Acts 2:24), and now that He has risen from the dead, He offers us a new life which is in Him. Those that are in Him will follow in His resurrection and be resurrected themselves with a new body someday (Romans 6:4-5). This is God's plan to save you. This is the Gospel of Jesus Christ, the Gospel of Salvation, the Good News about what Jesus did to save you! There is no other power and no other plan to save you.

Romans 1:16 For I am not ashamed of the gospel of Christ: for **it is the power of God unto salvation** to every one that believeth; to the Jew first, and also to the Greek.

Here are a couple examples of Peter and Paul preaching the Gospel in Acts.

Acts 10:39 And we are witnesses of all things which he did both in the land of the Jews, and in Jerusalem; **whom they slew and hanged on a tree:**

Acts 10:40 **Him God raised up the third day**, and shewed him openly;

Acts 10:43 To him give all the prophets witness, that **through his name whosoever believeth in him shall receive remission of sins.**

(Peter Preaching Acts 10)

Acts 13:28 And though they found no cause of death in him, yet desired they Pilate **that he should be slain.**

Acts 13:29 And when they had fulfilled all that was written of him, **they took him down from the tree, and laid him in a sepulchre.**

Acts 13:30 **But God raised him from the dead:**

Acts 13:38 Be it known unto you therefore, men and brethren, **that through this man is preached unto you the forgiveness of sins:**

Acts 13:39 And **by him all that believe are justified from all things,** from which ye could not be justified by the law of Moses.

(Paul Preaching Acts 13)

You say that's too simple, too easy, more must be required. I warn you don't add anything to this Gospel. If you add any work of the flesh to what Jesus did in order to save someone's soul, you are adding to the Gospel of Christ; you're adding in your filthy righteousness to the perfect life of Christ, and you are accursed of God. I say this to give you a warning, this is very serious, and sadly it's common in many churches today to add to, and pervert the Gospel.

Galatians 1:6 **I marvel that ye are so soon removed from him that called you into the grace of Christ unto another gospel:**
Galatians 1:7 Which is not another; but **there be some that trouble you, and would pervert the gospel of Christ.**
Galatians 1:8 But though we, or an angel from heaven, preach any other gospel unto you than that which we have preached unto you, let him be accursed.
Galatians 1:9 As we said before, so say I now again, **if any man preach any other gospel unto you than that ye have received, let him be accursed.**

To Summarize, Jesus died for our sins (because we are sinners and deserve to die), He was buried, and He rose from the dead the third day according to the scriptures. The phrase "according to the scriptures" is important because it emphasizes that this is in accordance with how the Old Testament scriptures describe. In other words, God in flesh died, was buried, and had a physical bodily resurrection as the scriptures describe. Various Cults say they believe the Gospel but it's not according to the scriptures. Jehovah's Witnesses deny Christ was God. Muslims believe in Jesus as a prophet but deny that He was God, and they also deny that He physically died and rose again. Now that you know what the Gospel message is, you need to know how to receive it. We'll look at this in the following chapters.

# The Parable of the Sower

Now that we are clear on what the Gospel of Salvation is, it's time to start looking at how this Gospel is applied to our souls. Jesus explains the Parable of the Sower to His Disciples in the Bible, and this parable is recorded in Matthew, Mark, and Luke. In the Bible, the Gospel of Salvation is sometimes referred to as the gospel, the word, the word of truth, the holy commandment, or a few other synoptic phrases. In the Parable of the Sower, it's referred to as the Word of the Kingdom-Matthew, the Word-Mark, and the Word of God-Luke, and in each case, the Word here in this parable is the Gospel of Salvation message, and is symbolized by a seed.

Jesus explains to us how that there are four types of hearts the seed will fall upon when the message is preached, and the four types of hearts are symbolized in the parable by four types of soil. We'll look at each of these types of soil because if you can understand this parable it will clear up some of the questions you may have about who does and doesn't receive salvation. It could also help you to examine your own heart to see if you have a heart that is capable of receiving the Word of God.

You must keep in mind that when the seed is sown it doesn't always produce a fruitful plant immediately, and so to be clear I am not saying that because someone appears to be a certain way now, they will never be saved. It's possible the seed could have been received but the increase hasn't taken place yet as Paul indicates in 1 Corinthians 3, stating that he planted the Gospel seeds and Apollos came afterward and watered the seeds. However, it is only God that will cause the growth (and we don't know what his timing is).

> 1 Corinthians 3:**6 I have planted, Apollos watered; but God gave the increase.**
>
> 1 Corinthians 3:7 So then neither is he that planteth any thing, neither he that watereth; but God that giveth the increase.

The first type of soil is bad soil that the seed never has a chance to get started in. Furthermore, on this type of ground, there are birds (Satan) that come and eat the seeds, so the message is taken away and doesn't stay in their heart. When the Gospel is heard by a person with this type of heart it has no impact. Most of the time they will think it's foolishness or even worse blasphemy. The person who has this type of heart will not profess to be a Christian. Some of these people will blaspheme Jesus and some will persecute Christians. Others will speak kindly of Jesus but will not believe in His power to save their souls. The next two types of soil/hearts will both profess to be Christians at some point. However, in both cases, we'll see they were never truly born again and never a true Child of God.

> Matthew 13:4 And when he sowed, some seeds fell by the way side, and the fowls came and devoured them up:

The second type of soil is a soil that is shallow and that is upon stony ground. Jesus says the people which have these types of hearts quickly and joyfully will receive the gospel message. With joy, they believe and will profess that they are Christians. This is very sad and tragic because these people eventually fall away from the faith. Jesus goes on to explain that these people were without a root, or in other words the message never truly took hold in their hearts. In a time of affliction or persecution, they become offended and fall away from Christ. These people don't have a true understanding of the Gospel. While they do believe a message about Jesus, it turns out the message that they thought they heard doesn't match the true one that was preached to them.

> Mark 4:16 And these are they likewise **which are sown on stony ground**; who, when they have heard the word, immediately receive it with gladness;
> Mark 4:17 **And have no root in themselves**, and so endure but for a time: afterward, when affliction or persecution ariseth for the word's sake, immediately they are offended.

Often these people are very religious, and they'll accept the gospel so long as they get to play a part in their salvation. However, when they discover that their good works are of no avail to helping get them into heaven, they will abandon ship and search for a more works-friendly religion. No better example of this can be found than of that in John Chapter 6. In this chapter, Jesus explains to some of his disciples that He alone is what will get them to eternal life.

> John 6:51 I am the living bread which came down from heaven: **if any man eat of this bread, he shall live for ever:** and the bread that I will give is my flesh, which I will give for the life of the world.
> John 6:52 The Jews therefore strove among themselves, saying, How can this man give us his flesh to eat?
> John 6:53 Then Jesus said unto them, Verily, verily, I say unto you, Except ye eat the flesh of the Son of man, and drink his blood, ye have no life in you.
> John 6:54 **Whoso eateth my flesh, and drinketh my blood, hath eternal life; and I will raise him up at the last day**.

Furthermore, He tells them that it's His Spirit that will give life, and what they do in their flesh will be of no profit to them whatsoever when it comes to attaining eternal life.

> John 6:63 **It is the spirit that quickeneth; the flesh profiteth nothing:** the words that I speak unto you, they are spirit, and they are life.

Sadly, after Jesus made this statement many of the disciples who had been following Him until that point became offended and no longer walked with Him. These are not the twelve, but other disciples who also followed Him. Now, the following statements that Jesus makes show us a couple important facts.

First, although they once professed a belief in Jesus, the belief they held was not a true saving belief. They had believed in their head, but they had not believed with all their heart which is what is required for true salvation.

> John 6:64 But there are some of you that believe not. **For Jesus knew from the beginning who they were that believed not, and who should betray him.**

Second, they were never truly called by the Father and given to the Son. They were never truly saved. Their issue was not that they failed to keep doing good works. Their issue was that they were never true believers in the first place. You see, He had just told them that no one can come to Him unless the Father draws them and that He would not cast out any who the Father gives Him.

---

John 6:37 All that the Father giveth me shall come to me; and him that cometh to me I will in no wise cast out.

John 6:44 **No man can come to me, except the Father which hath sent me draw him: and I will raise him up at the last day.**

(Back to verse 65)

John 6:65 And he said, **Therefore said I unto you, that no man can come unto me, except it were given unto him of my Father.**

John 6:66 From that time many of his disciples went back, and walked no more with him.

---

John explains to us in 1 John Chapter 2 that these people were never truly saved and that if they had been truly born again, and were with Us the true believers, they would have never left the faith. Notice, he says that if they were of us, they would have no doubt continued with us, in other words, there is no question here that the truly saved don't fall away. This isn't just John's opinion; this is the voice of the Holy Ghost. Likewise, the writer of Hebrews makes a separation between those who once professed a belief and those who had a true saving belief.

| 1 John 2:19 They went out from us, but they were not of us; **for if they had been of us, they would no doubt have continued with us**: but they went out, that they might be made manifest that they were not all of us. | Hebrews 10:38 Now the just shall live by faith: but if any man draw back, my soul shall have no pleasure in him.<br>Hebrews 10:39 **But we are not of them who draw back unto perdition; but of them that believe to the saving of the soul.** |
|---|---|

Some of these shallow-ground believers will only remain in the faith for a short while, but others may continue for some time. Some of these people are Pastors, Teachers, or Singers. Some may put on a very religious showing. They may have fooled you as well as themselves into thinking that they were the real deal, but when they fall away be assured, they were never in the family to begin with. To clarify, falling away is not falling away from your particular church or denomination, rather falling away biblically is falling away from faith in Christ. It's going from once professing faith in Jesus to no longer professing faith. This will become more and more prevalent as time goes on and we draw closer to the end.

| 1 Timothy 4:1 Now the Spirit speaketh expressly, **that in the latter times some shall depart from the faith,** giving heed to seducing spirits, and doctrines of devils; | 2 Thessalonians 2:3 Let no man deceive you by any means: **for that day shall not come, except there come a falling away first,** and that man of sin be revealed, the son of perdition; |
|---|---|

The third type of soil has thorns growing in it. Jesus says that when the seed falls on this type of soil it's received like as the soil on stony ground, but whereas the previous soil lacked depth and didn't allow for a root, this soil has thorns that choke the word. Jesus says that the cares of this world, and riches and pleasures, choke the word so that no fruit may be produced. The people who have this type of heart do receive the word but care more for this present life than for God. Like the previous soil, the word is received and grows a plant, but it's fruitless. Likewise, there is a head belief here but not a heart belief. These people will also proclaim to be Christians.

These people want Heaven and all its glory and riches, but they don't desire a true relationship with the Lord. They get into Christianity as someone purchases an insurance policy. Their religious life is nothing more than a fire assurance policy from Hell, or so they think. They don't understand that true salvation is a restoration of a Relationship with God, and all that comes with that. They think that because they repeated a prayer at one time in their life, God gave them a ticket to Heaven that they could hide away in their back pocket, with no intention of being a true disciple of Jesus, no intention of loving their neighbor as themselves, no intention of living a holy life separated from the filth of this world, and no desire for righteousness.

> Luke 8:14 **And that which fell among thorns** are they, which, when they have heard, go forth, and are choked with cares and riches and pleasures of this life, and bring no fruit to perfection.

They will say a lot of correct things and can tell you about how Jesus died for sinners. They'll also openly commit sin, and sometimes won't even be ashamed of it. They love to quote verses about not judging others. Their life is dominated by their lust and desires. They didn't become a "Christian" so that they could have a new life that is in fellowship with God. They are simply looking to benefit from what Jesus has to offer them, namely an escape from Hell. Peter speaks of some of these people in 2 Peter. He is specifically referring to false teachers in the verses below, and these false teachers have converts under them. If you read the entire chapter, you'll see that the main motivation for these people is money. I won't name any names here, but this chapter is a vivid description of many popular prosperity preachers of our time who live in multi-million dollar mansions, and who preach a perverted gospel.

2 Peter 2:10 But chiefly **them that walk after the flesh in the lust of uncleanness**, and despise government. Presumptuous are they, selfwilled, they are not afraid to speak evil of dignities.

2 Peter 2:12 But these, as natural brute beasts, made to be taken and destroyed, speak evil of the things that they understand not; and shall utterly perish in their own corruption;

2 Peter 2:13 And shall receive the reward of unrighteousness, as they that count it pleasure to riot in the day time. **Spots they are and blemishes, sporting themselves with their own deceivings while they feast with you;**

2 Peter 2:14 Having eyes full of adultery, and that cannot cease from sin; beguiling unstable souls: **an heart they have exercised with covetous practices; cursed children:**

In case we weren't sure if these people were truly saved or not, Peter makes it clear in verse 17 that these people are wells without water.

> 2 Peter 2:17 **These are wells without water**, clouds that are carried with a tempest; to whom the mist of darkness is reserved for ever.

The True Christian has a well of water within them that will never run dry.

> John 4:14 But whosoever drinketh of the water that I shall give him **shall never thirst; but the water that I shall give him shall be in him a well of water springing up into everlasting life.**

Jude also refers to these people. Jude says they are clouds without water, trees without fruit, and twice dead indicating they will suffer the second death.

> Jude 1:12 These are spots in your feasts of charity, when they feast with you, feeding themselves without fear: **clouds they are without water,** carried about of winds; trees whose fruit withereth, **without fruit, twice dead**, plucked up by the roots;
>
> Jude 1:16 **These are murmurers, complainers, walking after their own lusts**; and their mouth speaketh great swelling words, having men's persons in admiration because of advantage.

He further clarifies that these people do not have the Spirit of God.

> Jude 1:19 These be they who separate themselves, sensual, **having not the Spirit.**

The problem these people have is not that they couldn't stop sinning. The truth is, none of us are capable in our flesh, nor will we ever be completely free of sin as long as we are in the flesh. The difference between the born again and those who are not is in their desire to please the Lord, and this desire will manifest at least somewhat in our lives. You see, when Jesus died for us and took away our sins, He was doing more than just changing our real estate from Hell to Heaven. He was restoring what Adam lost when he sinned in the garden. What Jesus accomplished restores us to God and is a restoration of the relationship between God and man that was lost when Adam sinned. When you accept Jesus and Salvation, you must understand that it comes as a package deal. Heaven is wonderful and I'm thankful that God tells us of its beauty and splendor, but the prize of salvation is not Heaven nor an escape from Hell. The prize of Salvation is being reconciled back into a relationship with our Heavenly Father.

| 2 Corinthians 5:18 And all things are of God, **who hath reconciled us** to himself by Jesus Christ, and hath given to us **the ministry of reconciliation;** |
| --- |

That brings us to the final type of soil which is the good ground. When the Word of God is heard by people who have this type of heart, they receive it. The Word takes hold in their heart, and they are born again. These people may be murderers, prostitutes, or drug addicts, but what separates them from the previous group is that they are willing and desire to have a new life. These people will have the fruit of salvation in their lives, some more than others, but all will have some fruit.

> Mark 4:20 **And these are they which are sown on good ground;** such as hear the word, and receive it, **and bring forth fruit**, some thirtyfold, some sixty, and some an hundred.
>
> Luke 8:15 **But that on the good ground are they**, which in an honest and good heart, **having heard the word, keep it, and bring forth fruit** with patience.

What is this fruit you may ask? The fruit is what comes forth as a result of the Spirit of God living inside of us. This fruit is not religious practices such as church attendance, giving money, abstaining from drugs or alcohol, etc. While those practices are wise and beneficial to Christian living, the true Fruit of the Spirit is what is recorded in Galatians.

> Galatians 5:22 But **the fruit of the Spirit is love, joy, peace, longsuffering, gentleness, goodness, faith,**
> Galatians 5:23 **Meekness, temperance**: against such there is no law.

A good example of this fruit would be when an individual who is anxious and nervous by nature gets saved, and now they have peace, or when someone who was before violent gets saved, and now they show gentleness, someone previously cocky who is now meek, someone always depressed and now they have joy. Furthermore, when you are born again the Holy Spirit will now forever dwell with and in you. Because the Spirit of the Lord will be dwelling within you, He will give you light and Jesus says you shall not walk in darkness because you will have His light, not that you might not, but that you shall not.

> John 8:12 Then spake Jesus again unto them, saying, I am the light of the world: **he that followeth me shall not walk in darkness, but shall have the light of life.**

God tells us about His New Covenant in the Old Testament and explains how those who are joined to Him in this covenant will be given a new heart, and that He will cause them to follow Him. He also says that they will know Him.

| | |
|---|---|
| Jeremiah 31:33 **But this shall be the covenant that I will make with the house of Israel;** After those days, saith the LORD, **I will put my law in their inward parts, and write it in their hearts;** and will be their God, and they shall be my people. | Hebrews 8:10 **For this is the covenant that I will make with the house of Israel after those days, saith the Lord; I will put my laws into their mind, and write them in their hearts:** and I will be to them a God, and they shall be to me a people: |
| Jeremiah 31:34 And they shall teach no more every man his neighbour, and every man his brother, saying, Know the LORD: **for they shall all know me, from the least of them unto the greatest of them,** saith the LORD: for **I will forgive their iniquity, and I will remember their sin no more.** | Hebrews 8:11 And they shall not teach every man his neighbour, and every man his brother, saying, Know the Lord: **for all shall know me, from the least to the greatest.**<br><br>(The last part of verse 11 excludes anyone to whom the Lord will say "I never knew you" from ever being a True Christian) |

We are also told in Ezekial that God is going to put a new spirit within us, and we find out in the New Testament that this is the Holy Spirit.

| | |
|---|---|
| Ezekiel 36:25 **Then will I sprinkle clean water upon you, and ye shall be clean**: from all your filthiness, and from all your idols, will I cleanse you. | Hebrews 10:22 Let us draw near with a true heart in full assurance of faith, **having our hearts sprinkled from an evil conscience, and our bodies washed with pure water**. |
| Ezekiel 36:26 **A new heart also will I give you, and a new spirit will I put within you**: and I will take away the stony heart out of your flesh, and I will give you an heart of flesh. | John 14:17 Even **the Spirit of truth**; whom the world cannot receive, because it seeth him not, neither knoweth him: but ye know him; **for he dwelleth with you, and shall be in you.** |
| Ezekiel 36:27 And I will put my spirit within you, **and cause you to walk in my statutes, and ye shall keep my judgments, and do them.** | 2 Corinthians 3:3 Forasmuch as ye are manifestly declared to be the epistle of Christ ministered by us, **written not with ink, but with the Spirit of the living God; not in tables of stone, but in fleshy tables of the heart.** |

God is seeking to save all those who are open to having a relationship with Him. He will do all the work. You don't have to figure out how to overcome your sins, and you don't have to try to clean up before you call out to God. When the Spirit of God comes into your soul, He'll start the cleanup and the restoration. You just need to understand and be open to the fact that once He comes in, He Will be working in your life, and you will have a brand-new life!

# The Curse of the Law

When Moses led the children of Israel out of Egypt, and they came to Sinai, God instructed him to tell the people that if they would obey Him and keep His covenant, they would be a Kingdom of Priest and a Holy Nation. We also find later that one of God's purposes for Israel was that by being a Holy Nation they should be a light to all the other Nations who would look at them and would see that God was with Israel. God wanted Israel to be His Witness to all the other nations that He was the True God. That is why there were such strict punishments in some cases such as being killed if you committed adultery or worshiped another god. God was very serious about Israel being set apart from the rest of the Nations and being His witness.

| | |
|---|---|
| Deuteronomy 4:6 Keep therefore and do them; for this is your wisdom and your understanding in the sight **of the nations, which shall hear all these statutes, and say, Surely this great nation is a wise and understanding people.** | Isaiah 43:10 **Ye are my witnesses,** saith the LORD, and my servant whom I have chosen: that ye may know and believe me, and understand that I am he: before me there was no God formed, neither shall there be after me. |
| Deuteronomy 4:7 **For what nation is there so great, who hath God so nigh unto them**, as the LORD our God is in all things that we call upon him for? | Isaiah 43:12 I have declared, and have saved, and I have shewed, when there was no strange god among you: therefore **ye are my witnesses, saith the LORD, that I am God.** |

The first Commandments that God gives Israel is the 10 Commandments. God came down upon Mount Sinai in a massive show of His glory and spoke the 10 Commandments. The 10 Commandments served as the basis of the First Covenant between God and the Nation of Israel. This was a National Covenant whereby Israel would be in God's favor and receive His blessings in the land that He was bringing them into. There was no promise given of eternal life to an individual for keeping the 10 Commandments. Now, when God came down on the mountain it was a fearful and awesome sight! It scared the people to death! It scared them so bad that they told Moses that going forward they wanted God to just speak to him and he could relay the messages back to them because they thought if God spoke to them again, they might die.

> Exodus 20:19 And they said unto Moses, Speak thou with us, and we will hear: but let not God speak with us, lest we die.

Furthermore, they told Moses to relay a message to God and say-whatever God wants us to do we'll do it!

> Deuteronomy 5:27 Go thou near, and hear all that the LORD our God shall say: and speak thou unto us all that the LORD our God shall speak unto thee; and **we will hear it, and do it.**

When Moses told God what the people said, God spoke to Moses and told him He approved of what they had said. However, we also see from God's response that He knows they are not going to be able to hold up their part of the bargain.

> Deuteronomy 5:28 And the LORD heard the voice of your words, when ye spake unto me; and the LORD said unto me, I have heard the voice of the words of this people, which they have spoken unto thee: **they have well said all that they have spoken.**
>
> Deuteronomy 5:29 **O that there were such an heart in them, that they would fear me, and keep all my commandments always**, that it might be well with them, and with their children for ever!

The Book of Deuteronomy is known as the Book of the Law in the Bible. The entire Old Testament is often referred to as the Law. There are also other laws in other books. However, when it specifically says the Book of the Law, it's referring to Deuteronomy. Moses wrote Deuteronomy just before he died and before the people crossed the Jordan. The laws laid out in this book (or any other book) were not to be added to and not to be taken away from.

| | |
|---|---|
| Deuteronomy 4:2 **Ye shall not add unto the word which I command you, neither shall ye diminish ought from it**, that ye may keep the commandments of the LORD your God which I command you. | Matthew 5:18 For verily I say unto you, **Till heaven and earth pass, one jot or one tittle shall in no wise pass from the law**, till all be fulfilled. |
| Deuteronomy 12:32 What thing soever I command you, observe to do it: **thou shalt not add thereto, nor diminish from it.** | Matthew 24:35 Heaven and earth shall pass away, **but my words shall not pass away.** |

In Chapter 11 of Deuteronomy, God tells us that The Law is both a blessing and a curse. In Chapter 27, He says that anyone who fails to confirm the words of the law by doing it is Cursed, all of it!

Deuteronomy 11:26 Behold, **I set before you this day a blessing and a curse;**

Deuteronomy 27:26 **Cursed be he that confirmeth not all the words of this law to do them.** And all the people shall say, Amen.

The Apostle Paul pulls from this verse in Galatians and explains that everyone (everyone under the law) who doesn't keep the whole law is Cursed!

Galatians 3:10 For as many as are of the works of the law are under the curse: **for it is written, Cursed is every one that continueth not in all things which are written in the book of the law to do them.**

God reminds Israel through the prophet Jeremiah of the covenant and the curse in Chapter 11 of Jeremiah.

> Jeremiah 11:3 And say thou unto them, Thus saith the LORD God of Israel; **Cursed be the man that obeyeth not the words of this covenant,**

When the Jews returned to Judea after the Babylonian exile, they made another oath to God saying they were going to obey all His Commandments, Judgements, and Statutes. God's Word tells us that when they did this, they entered into a Curse!

> Nehemiah 10:29 They clave to their brethren, their nobles, **and entered into a curse, and into an oath, to walk in God's law**, which was given by Moses the servant of God, and to observe and do all the commandments of the LORD our Lord, and his judgments and his statutes;

You see when the children of Israel told God that they would do whatever He said, they were making a boast that they didn't understand. They had no idea how Holy God is, nor did they understand that He requires sinless perfection. God told them what He requires in Deuteronomy Chapter 10.

> Deuteronomy 10:12 And now, Israel, **what doth the LORD thy God require of thee, but to fear the LORD thy God, <u>to walk in all his ways</u>, and to love him, and to serve the LORD thy God with all thy heart and with all thy soul,**

God's requirements to be in relationship with Him according to the law:

Fear God

Walk in all God's ways

Love God

Serve God with all your heart and soul

Keep God's commandments and statutes – "All of Them"

When David wrote Psalm 119 (through the inspiration of the Holy Ghost) he understood that those who keep the law are Blessed. David writes Psalm 119 and goes on and on about the Blessings of keeping God's law. Psalm 119 is the longest chapter in the Bible. The Psalm starts out by declaring how that those who walk in God's law are Blessed.

Psalm 119:1 **Blessed are the undefiled in the way, who walk in the law of the LORD.**

Psalm 119:2 Blessed are they that keep his testimonies, and that seek him with the whole heart.

Psalm 119:3 They also do no iniquity: they walk in his ways.

Psalm 119:4 **Thou hast commanded us to keep thy precepts diligently.**

However, at the end of Psalm 119, David comes to a sad conclusion. While he loves God's law and realizes that it is holy and righteous, he also realizes his inability to keep it perfectly. David understands that he is in a lost condition according to the demands of the law.

David knows that he missed the mark of perfection and cries out to the Lord to save him because he went astray as a lost sheep. The true Christian is just like David in Psalm 119. We understand the law is holy and good, but we also understand we can never live up to its demands perfectly. We understand that we've fallen short and gone astray and have cried out for help just like David did. In our flesh, we are all Cursed with no hope.

> Psalm 119:176 **I have gone astray like a lost sheep**; seek thy servant; for I do not forget thy commandments.

As I said, we have all gone astray just like David did.

> Isaiah 53:6 **All we like sheep have gone astray**; we have turned every one to his own way; and the LORD hath laid on him the iniquity of us all.

However, God promised that He would come and seek out His sheep that had gone astray. At the same time, He would destroy the fat and strong ones. These are the ones that didn't realize they had gone astray and thought they were capable of following His laws, and who thought they were already in the right condition.

> Ezekiel 34:11 For thus saith the Lord GOD; Behold, **I, even I, will both search my sheep, and seek them out.**
>
> Ezekiel 34:16 **I will seek that which was lost,** and bring again that which was driven away, and will bind up that which was broken, and will strengthen that which was sick: **but I will destroy the fat and the strong; I will feed them with judgment.**

Jesus came and He told us that He is the Shepard.

> John 10:14 I am the good shepherd, and know my sheep, and am known of mine.

Jesus gave His life for His Sheep.

> John 10:11 I am the good shepherd: **the good shepherd giveth his life for the sheep.**

By giving His life the Good Shepard returned the sheep that went astray.

> 1 Peter 2:25 **For ye were as sheep going astray; but are now returned** unto the Shepherd and Bishop of your souls.
>
> Psalm 23:1 **The LORD is my shepherd**; I shall not want.

Now, in order to return the sheep Jesus had to do what the sheep could not. Jesus lived a perfect life and fulfilled all the demands of the law. He did not change the law, but He fulfilled it perfectly. He lived in complete accordance with it.

> Matthew 5:17 Think not that I am come to destroy the law, or the prophets: **I am not come to destroy, but to fulfil.**

Jesus took our place and took our Curse upon Himself. Because of what He did, He freed us from the Curse so that God can now offer us salvation and bless us even though we have failed to keep the law.

> Galatians 3:13 **Christ hath redeemed us from the curse of the law, being made a curse for us**: for it is written, Cursed is every one that hangeth on a tree:

If you've been saved and are no longer trusting in your ability to uphold the demands of the law, but are trusting in Jesus, you are now **Blessed**. To Trust the Lord is to rely upon Him totally to save you. The Blessed are not trusting in their ability to keep the law because they know they cannot keep it perfectly. The law has been their schoolmaster to bring them to Christ (Galatians 3:24) and has taught them that they are unable to live up to God's standards. Furthermore, the Blessed will never cease from yielding fruit as is said in Jeremiah 17.

---

Jeremiah 17:7 **Blessed is the man that trusteth in the LORD**, and whose hope the LORD is.

Jeremiah 17:18 **For he shall be as a tree planted by the waters**, and that spreadeth out her roots by the river, and shall not see when heat cometh, but her leaf shall be green; and shall not be careful in the year of drought, **neither shall cease from yielding fruit**.

---

We are also told in the Psalms how those who Trust in The Lord are Blessed.

---

| Psalm 2:12 Kiss the Son, lest he be angry, and ye perish from the way, when his wrath is kindled but a little. **Blessed are all they that put their trust in him.** | Psalm 34:8 O taste and see that the LORD is good: **blessed is the man that trusteth in him.** |
|---|---|

The Blessed have had their sins covered by the Blood of Jesus. Though the Blessed have iniquity, the Lord does not impute or charge it to their account. The Blessed receives their blessing based totally upon what Jesus did, and their only contribution is to Trust that what Jesus did was enough to save them.

| | |
|---|---|
| Psalm 32:1 **Blessed is he whose transgression is forgiven**, whose sin is covered.<br><br>Psalm 32:2 **Blessed is the man unto whom the LORD imputeth not iniquity**, and in whose spirit there is no guile. | Romans 4:6 Even as David also describeth **the blessedness of the man, unto whom God imputeth righteousness without works,**<br>Romans 4:7 Saying, **Blessed are they whose iniquities are forgiven, and whose sins are covered.**<br>Romans 4:8 **Blessed is the man to whom the Lord will not impute sin.** |

Jesus earned the Blessing through His perfect life. We are Blessed when we are found in Him. You will be found in Jesus when you put all your trust in Him, not in your ability to keep the law but trust alone in what He did for you.

| |
|---|
| Ephesians 1:3 Blessed be the God and Father of our Lord Jesus Christ, **who hath blessed us with all spiritual blessings in heavenly places in Christ:** |

Have you been Blessed through Christ, or are you still under the Curse of the Law?

# A Perfect Righteousness

It's very important that you understand that Righteousness is required in order to enter the Kingdom of God. To be righteous basically means that you are in a right standing or position morally. Another word you could substitute for righteous in most cases would be Just, as in Justified. The World has its own definition of what is righteous or morally correct, but when we're talking about righteousness as a Christian, we are speaking of being in a right standing with God. God is who defines what is right and wrong. While a non-believer can perform righteous acts such as giving to the poor, helping widows and orphans (all things God approves of), they can't ultimately be Righteous before God because of their sin.

There has been a lot of confusion amongst people of all beliefs in that some believe that being a Christian and trusting totally in Christ, means that we believe that righteousness is not important to God and not required for salvation. That is completely false. What these opponents fail to realize is that the True Christian is the one who establishes the law and is who establishes righteousness.

Romans 3:31 Do we then make void the law through faith? God forbid: yea, **we establish the law.**

An Opponent to Grace through Faith doesn't understand that God requires absolute Perfection. They have bought into the lie of religion that has told them that God judges on a grade and if they score a certain score on the scale of righteousness they'll pass, and if they don't, they'll fail. As if their life is a test and if they can score above 70% or so they'll pass and be allowed into Heaven. In order to enter God's presence nothing short of 100% is going to give you a pass.

In the Gospels, Jesus preaches both Perfect Performance and Perfect Trust. If you don't understand this, you will be confused when reading your Bible. You will read verses where He tells people they will be saved by their Faith and through Belief, and then you will read verses where He tells people they must have a Perfect Righteousness. If you don't understand what's going on, you'll ultimately choose which verses you want to ignore and which you want to concentrate on. If you're religious you'll love the verses about being righteous and ignore those that show salvation comes by faith, and if you're liberal you'll ignore the verses on righteousness and only focus on verses that speak of God's love.

In the Sermon on the Mount, Jesus goes through a list of "Ye have heard it said but I say" verses in which He explains that God not only judges people based upon actions that they physically carry out but that He also judges people based upon what is in their heart.

While some believe Jesus is introducing a totally new concept, He is actually reiterating what was already told in the Old Testament.

| | |
|---|---|
| Matthew 5:21 Ye have heard that it was said of them of old time, Thou shalt not kill; and whosoever shall kill shall be in danger of the judgment:<br>Matthew 5:22 **But I say unto you, That whosoever is angry with his brother without a cause shall be in danger of the judgment:** and whosoever shall say to his brother, Raca, shall be in danger of the council: but whosoever shall say, Thou fool, shall be in danger of hell fire. | Leviticus 19:17 **Thou shalt not hate thy brother in thine heart:** thou shalt in any wise rebuke thy neighbour, and not suffer sin upon him.<br>Leviticus 19:18 **Thou shalt not avenge, nor bear any grudge against the children of thy people,** but thou shalt love thy neighbour as thyself: I am the LORD. |

At the end of His sermon, Jesus tells us to be therefore Perfect. When you see the word "Therefore" you must understand that what follows therefore is based on facts or evidence that has been previously provided. In this case, what Jesus is saying is that in order to get to Heaven you must be Perfect both in deed and thought. I've heard people try to explain this verse before and they've stated that Jesus couldn't actually mean we must be perfect (because they knew none of us can be and that wasn't possible). They went on to explain that it means you must do the best you can. However, the end of the verse makes that explanation impossible. You see, Jesus tells us to be Perfect even as our Father in Heaven is Perfect. In other words, be Perfect in the same way God is Perfect. God is completely and totally Perfect, the definition of Perfection. To even compare our perfection to His is blasphemy.

> Matthew 5:48 Be ye therefore perfect, **even as your Father which is in heaven is perfect.**

But even this statement that Jesus made about being perfect was not a new idea, because it had been spoken in the law already.

| Deuteronomy 18:13 **Thou shalt be perfect** with the LORD thy God. | Proverbs 2:21 For the upright shall dwell in the land, and **the perfect shall remain in it.** |
|---|---|

God's law is Perfect. The problem is we are not. Therefore, the law cannot save us. So, the problem is not that the law is flawed but that we are. If we could follow the law, we would be perfect.

| Psalm 19:7 **The law of the LORD is perfect,** converting the soul: the testimony of the LORD is sure, making wise the simple. | Hebrews 7:19 **For the law made nothing perfect**, but the bringing in of a better hope did; by the which we draw nigh unto God. |
|---|---|

In 3 of the 4 Gospels, we read about the story of the Rich Young Ruler. This story shows us what God thinks about our righteousness and it shows us what is required. First, we see the Rich Young Ruler come to Jesus and address Him as Good Master. No doubt he is surprised by the response he receives from Jesus when Jesus asks him why he called Him Good. Then, Jesus says that no one is Good except for God. Before we go any further, understand Jesus is not saying that He is not Good.

JESUS IS GOD AND HE IS GOOD. However, he is not approaching Jesus as God. The rich young ruler is approaching Jesus as just another Rabbi, another religious leader. So, Jesus is going to let him know that he (the young man) is not good and that Perfection is required. You see, the young man wants to know what he has to do in his flesh to go to heaven and to inherit eternal life.

> Luke 18:18 And a certain ruler asked him, saying, Good Master, **what shall I do to inherit eternal life?**

Jesus tells him there is no one Good but God, but if he wants to have eternal life, he must keep the commandments. He lists some of the 10 Commandments but also includes "Love thy Neighbour as Thyself" from Leviticus.

> Matthew 19:17 And he said unto him, Why callest thou me good? **there is none good but one, that is, God: but if thou wilt enter into life, keep the commandments.**
>
> Matthew 19:18 He saith unto him, Which? Jesus said, Thou shalt do no murder, Thou shalt not commit adultery, Thou shalt not steal, Thou shalt not bear false witness,
>
> Matthew 19:19 Honour thy father and thy mother: **and, Thou shalt love thy neighbour as thyself.**

The Young Man responds to Jesus and tells Him that he has kept the commandments since he was young. Personally, I don't think he had, but it's irrelevant because Jesus wants to address a particular sin that the young man had which was covetousness, and for not distributing to the poor the way he should.

You see, Jesus didn't give him an exhaustive list but rather a summary of the law. The law also commands that you must lend to and help the poor.

| Matthew 19:21 Jesus said unto him, **If thou wilt be perfect**, go and sell that thou hast, and give to the poor, and thou shalt have treasure in heaven: and come and follow me. | Deuteronomy 15:7 **If there be among you a poor man** of one of thy brethren within any of thy gates in thy land which the LORD thy God giveth thee, thou shalt not harden thine heart, nor shut thine hand from thy poor brother: Deuteronomy 15:8 But **thou shalt open thine hand wide unto him, and shalt surely lend him sufficient for his need,** in that which he wanteth. |

The Young Man went away from Jesus sad. Jesus didn't try to stop him or tell him to put his trust in Him. The message that Jesus has for those who rely on religion to save them is that it won't. The Pharisees were the most strict and religious people alive. Any religion you have witnessed in your life would pale in comparison to that of the Pharisees, yet it was not perfect and therefore could not get them into heaven.

Matthew 5:20 For I say unto you, That **except your righteousness shall exceed the righteousness of the scribes and Pharisees, ye shall in no case enter into the kingdom of heaven.**

You see, God tells us in Deuteronomy that our righteousness towards Him will be in accordance to keeping His commandments. So, that means if we've broken any of the commandments, we are unable to be counted righteous because God is Perfect. According to our flesh, we are all unrighteous in the sight of God. That is why Isaiah tells us that our righteousness is like filthy rags.

| Deuteronomy 6:25 And it shall be **our righteousness, if we observe** to do all these commandments before the LORD our God, as he hath commanded us. | Isaiah 64:6 But we are all as an unclean thing, and **all our righteousnesses are as filthy rags**; and we all do fade as a leaf; and our iniquities, like the wind, have taken us away. |
| --- | --- |

God gives a warning to anyone trusting in their own righteousness in Ezekiel. God tells us that if a man is righteous before Him and then that man sins, all the righteousness that the man had before that will mean nothing! However, God also says that a Wicked person could find forgiveness if he were able to become righteous.

| Ezekiel 33:12 Therefore, thou son of man, say unto the children of thy people, **The righteousness of the righteous shall not deliver him in the day of his transgression:** as for the wickedness of the wicked, he shall not fall thereby in the day that he turneth from his wickedness; neither shall the righteous be able to live for his righteousness in the day that he sinneth. | Ezekiel 33:13 When I shall say to the righteous, that he shall surely live; **if he trust to his own righteousness**, and commit iniquity, **all his righteousnesses shall not be remembered**; but for his iniquity that he hath committed, he shall die for it. |
| --- | --- |

God further explains that in order for the Wicked to find forgiveness he would need to make an atonement for his wrongdoing and then he would need to live righteously going forward.

> Ezekiel 33:15 <u>If the wicked</u> **restore the pledge, give again that he had robbed, walk in the statutes of life, <u>without committing iniquity</u>; he shall surely live, he shall not die.**

Now, that's still a huge problem for a sinner because even if he were able to offer an appeasement for all his sins, he would still never be able to keep the law perfectly going forward. However, in Genesis, before the law and the commandments, we see something amazing. We see that God is willing to declare someone righteous when they put their trust in Him.

| | |
|---|---|
| Genesis 15:6 And **he believed in the LORD; and he counted it to him for righteousness.** | Romans 4:3 For what saith the scripture? **Abraham believed God, and it was counted unto him for righteousness.** Romans 4:5 But to him that worketh not, **but believeth** on him that justifieth the ungodly, **his faith is counted for righteousness.** |

How can God treat us as if we are righteous when we aren't you may ask? Well, God knew from the beginning that we couldn't be righteous in our flesh. That is why the Son of God came, and this was the plan God had made before the creation of the world.

You may have never heard this, but God will not forgive any sin. God is a Perfect Judge and for Him to be perfectly Just He must punish all sin. He will not forgive sin and He will not be in the presence of any sin whatsoever. God would be unjust if He sent anyone to Hell because of their sin but let you into Heaven because you had slightly less sin or just because you had said you were sorry. God says in Proverbs that a judge who justifies the wicked commits an abomination.

Proverbs 17:15 **He that justifieth the wicked**, and he that condemneth the just, even they both are **abomination to the LORD**.

You see, if a criminal had broken into your house and hurt your family, let's say the criminal murdered one of your family members, and then when the criminal was before the judge, the criminal said he was sorry, and the judge let him go free. You would be outraged! You would demand justice and would declare that the judge was evil. Well, because of our sins and the hurt we've caused each other and a Holy God, He will not forgive us. His Justice demands that our sins be punished. So, what God did is He offered a Propitiation.

Another word similar to propitiation and more common in modern language is appeasement. A propitiation or appeasement is something that an offending party offers the one who has been offended or wronged in order to make amends or atone for the damage that was done. This is what is so Amazing about the Gospel! God was the One offended and yet He is the One who offers us a Propitiation! Because of Jesus, we can once again be righteous or in a right standing with God!

| | |
|---|---|
| Romans 3:21 But now the **righteousness of God without the law is manifested**, being witnessed by the law and the prophets; Romans 3:22 **Even the righteousness of God which is by faith of Jesus Christ** unto all and **upon all them that believe:** for there is no difference: | Romans 3:25 **Whom God hath set forth to be a propitiation through faith in his blood**, to declare his righteousness for the remission of sins that are past, through the forbearance of God; Romans 3:26 To declare, I say, at this time his righteousness: **that he might be just,** and the justifier of him which believeth in Jesus. |
| 1 John 2:2 And **he is the propitiation for our sins**: and not for ours only, but also for the sins of the whole world. | 1 John 4:10 Herein is love, not that we loved God, but that **he loved us, and sent his Son to be the propitiation for our sins.** |

This is why God always required a sacrifice to atone for sins, and as it says in Hebrews, without the shedding of blood, there is no remission or removal of sins. You must never forget that any righteousness you have with God is only through the blood of Jesus, and any forgiveness of sins that you may have received is based strictly upon His blood and through the Propitiation.

Ephesians 1:7 In whom **we have redemption through his blood, the forgiveness of sins**, according to the riches of his grace;

The Lord is our righteousness. You are not righteous in your flesh. Going to church, praying, reading your Bible, giving to the poor, none of this can make you righteous with God. There are righteous deeds that God approves of and that we should do, but they don't make us righteous because we still have sin.

This was revealed to the Prophets in the Old Testament, but Israel had moved away from it at the time of Jesus.

| | |
|---|---|
| Jeremiah 23:6 In his days Judah shall be saved, and Israel shall dwell safely: and this is his name whereby he shall be called, **THE LORD OUR RIGHTEOUSNESS.** | Jeremiah 33:16 In those days shall Judah be saved, and Jerusalem shall dwell safely: and this is the name wherewith she shall be called, **The LORD our righteousness.** |

When you are saved, you will not declare your own righteousness, nor will you have any faith in it. You will understand that all your righteousness is of the Lord just as it says in Isaiah.

> Isaiah 54:17 No weapon that is formed against thee shall prosper; and every tongue that shall rise against thee in judgment thou shalt condemn. This is the heritage of the servants of the LORD, **and their righteousness is of me, saith the LORD.**

God credits the Believer with all the righteousness of Christ which is a Perfect Righteousness. This is the only way you can be saved.

> 2 Corinthians 5:21 For **he hath made him to be sin for us**, who knew no sin; **that we might be made the righteousness of God in him**.

If you're trying to establish your own righteousness you are headed for damnation. Paul speaks of this in Romans and explains that Christ is the end of trying to be righteous according to the law in order to be saved, for the true believer.

> Romans 10:4 For **Christ is the end of the law for righteousness to every one that believeth.**

However, if you are still trying to get into Heaven through your own righteousness, you have not yet submitted to God's righteousness and would therefore be damned unless you repent.

> Romans 10:3 For they <u>being ignorant of God's righteousness</u>, and **going about to establish their own righteousness, have not submitted** themselves unto the righteousness of God.

We must trust totally in Jesus for our salvation and rely completely upon Him.

> Philippians 3:9 And **be found in him, not having mine own righteousness, which is of the law**, but that which is through the faith of Christ, **the righteousness which is of God by faith**:

The Holy Ghost spoke of the coming High Priest in Psalms and compared Him to Melchizedek of whom Abraham had offered tithes to in Genesis. Hebrews shows us that if the law could have made anyone perfect there would have been no need for this High Priest to come.

| Psalm 110:4 The LORD hath sworn, and will not repent, Thou art a priest for ever after the order of Melchizedek. | Hebrews 7:11 If therefore **perfection** were by the Levitical priesthood, **(for under it the people received the law,)** what further need was there that another priest should rise after the order of Melchisedec, and not be called after the order of Aaron? |
|---|---|

Jesus is our prophesied High Priest that came after the order of Melchizedek and He has made the Perfect sacrifice for our sins, by which we can receive the atonement and become Perfected.

Hebrews 10:14 For by one offering **he hath perfected** for ever them that are sanctified.

You can be Perfectly Righteous in Jesus. You can join the assembly of people who have been Justified by His blood and made Perfect in the sight of God.

Hebrews 12:23 To the general assembly and church of the firstborn, which are written in heaven, and to God the Judge of all, and **to the spirits of just men made perfect,**

You can someday be presented to God as a Perfect Person who is perfectly acceptable in His sight.

Colossians 1:28 Whom we preach, warning every man, and teaching every man in all wisdom; **that we may present every man perfect in Christ Jesus:**

Have you accepted the Perfect Righteousness of Christ or are you still trying to establish your own?

# Garments of Different Sorts

God gives what seems to be a strange command in His law and He tells us not to mix garments of different sorts of material such as wool and linen together. When I used to read the Bible and come across these types of verses, if I'm honest I would think that God was being a little overly strict and giving some commands that didn't have any real benefit. I've since come to learn that God always has good reasons for His commandments and that usually when you see something like this that may appear strange, there is a deeper meaning behind it. This is the case with this commandment.

Deuteronomy 22:11 Thou shalt not wear a garment of divers sorts, as of woollen and linen together.

In the Bible, garments or clothing is used to represent a covering for sin. The first garments that man wore were made by Adam and Eve after they ate the forbidden fruit in the garden. When they realized they were naked they sewed fig leaves together to hide their nakedness.

However, we see that this fig leaf garment was not sufficient because after God addresses their sin, He then makes them coats of skins to wear. You see, man has never been able to cover his own sin. From the beginning, we have had to rely on God to cover and to clothe us.

Wool makes a nice warm garment, but it is often associated with work. Linen, however, is portrayed as God's fabric of choice for His priest and for His saints.

| | |
|---|---|
| Ezekiel 44:17 And it shall come to pass, that when they enter in at the gates of the inner court, **they shall be clothed with linen garments; and no wool shall come upon them**, whiles they minister in the gates of the inner court, and within. | Revelation 19: And to her was granted that **she should be arrayed in fine linen, clean and white: for the fine linen is the righteousness of saints.** |

Now, God tells us that we need to be clothed in Righteousness.

| | |
|---|---|
| Job 29:14 **I put on righteousness, and it clothed me**: my judgment was as a robe and a diadem. | Psalm 132:**9 Let thy priests be clothed with righteousness**; and let thy saints shout for joy. |

Before we are saved, we are like Adam and Eve. We try to cover our sins with our own righteousness. However, just as in their case, our covering is not sufficient, and God will not accept it. When a person is saved, God gives them a change of clothing and clothes them in His righteousness.

> Zechariah 3:4 And he answered and spake unto those that stood before him, saying, **Take away the filthy garments from him**. And unto him he said, Behold, **I have caused thine iniquity to pass from thee, and I will clothe thee with change of raiment**.

The new clothing that God gives us when we are saved is a robe of righteousness and is referred to as the Garment of Salvation.

> Isaiah 61:10 I will greatly rejoice in the LORD, my soul shall be joyful in my God; **for he hath clothed me with the garments of salvation**, he **hath covered me with the robe of righteousness**, as a bridegroom decketh himself with ornaments, and as a bride adorneth herself with her jewels.

Now, the problem occurs when we try to mix our own righteousness with Christ's Perfect Righteousness, and when we make salvation a shared accomplishment between Christ's finished work and our own works in the flesh. To some, Jesus is necessary for salvation but He's not sufficient. In other words, you may recognize the fact that Jesus had to die for you, but instead of totally trusting in what He did as your only means of salvation, you include yourself and your works. You might think that Jesus paid the downpayment, but now it's up to you to get in line and be righteous in order to keep yourself in a saved condition. This is extremely dangerous and is not how salvation works. You see, if our works and our own righteousness are involved in getting us to glory then Jesus died in vain.

> Galatians 2:21 I do not frustrate the grace of God: **for if righteousness come by the law, then Christ is dead in vain**.

It is only through Jesus that God accepts us as righteous. When you involve your own righteousness in salvation you contaminate it. To be clear, I am not saying we shouldn't try to live righteously! In fact, if you're truly saved you will want to live holy and to please God. What I'm talking about is trusting in your own righteousness and making it involved in your salvation and in keeping you saved. In other words, making your righteousness a cause and not the effect. I wouldn't be telling you this if it wasn't important.

In Galatians, Paul warns the Galatian church about adding works to the Gospel of Christ. Now, he is speaking to a church that he founded, but since the time Paul founded the church there had been people who had come in and told the Galatians that in order to stay saved, they had to not only believe in Jesus, but they also had to be circumcised according to the Old Testament precept.

Galatians 3:3 O foolish Galatians, **who hath bewitched you**, that ye should not obey the truth, before whose eyes Jesus Christ hath been evidently set forth, crucified among you?

Galatians 3:2 This only would I learn of you, Received ye the Spirit by the works of the law, or by the hearing of faith?

Galatians 3:3 **Are ye so foolish? having begun in the Spirit, are ye now made perfect by the flesh?**

Paul goes on to tell us that if you add works to your Salvation, Christ will not benefit you.

Galatians 5:2 Behold, I Paul say unto you, that **if ye be circumcised, Christ shall profit you nothing**.

You see, you must accept Salvation as God offers it and He offers it only by Grace. Salvation is based completely off what Jesus did for you. If you include any law, then you must include the entire law. God will not let you pick and choose which laws you can adhere to and which ones you can exclude. That is why Paul tells the Galatians that if they want to include Circumcision in their Salvation method they must include the entire law.

Galatians 5:3 For I testify again to every man that is circumcised, **that he is a debtor to do the whole law.**

The Apostle James echoes this message in his epistle.

James 2:10 For whosoever shall keep the whole law, and **yet offend in one point, he is guilty of all**.

People who want to argue that a person can lose their salvation will often quote a verse in Galatians that mentions falling from Grace as proof text that one can lose their salvation. However, I've never heard anyone who is making this point quote the entire verse. The reason they don't quote the entire verse is because if they knew what the verse was saying they would realize that they are guilty of the very thing that would cause someone to fall from grace, which is adding works to Justification. Paul doesn't say they lost their salvation at all. What he's saying is that some of these Galatians had moved away from Salvation by Grace Alone and had begun involving works. In doing so they had fallen from standing in the position that they originally held, and that Paul had preached.

> Galatians 5:4 **Christ is become of no effect unto you, <u>whosoever of you are justified by the law</u>; ye are fallen from grace**.

The implication is that while Paul had preached the true Gospel to them, by moving away from it, it indicated that some who originally agreed with Paul were not truly born again. This caused Paul to doubt that some of them were saved.

> Galatians 4:11 I am afraid of you, **lest I have bestowed upon you labour in vain.**

The only thing that will get you to Glory is Faith. We are in the last days and distortion of the gospel will become more and more prevalent.

> Galatians 5:6 For in Jesus Christ **neither circumcision availeth any thing, nor uncircumcision; but faith which worketh by love.**
>
> Galatians 5:7 Ye did run well; **who did hinder you that ye should not obey the truth?**
> Galatians 5:8 This persuasion cometh not of him that calleth you.

As far as adding Works to Grace, Paul wanted to "nip this in the bud" because he knew it would destroy the Galatian church.

> Galatians 5:9 A little leaven leaveneth the whole lump.

Anyone who perverts the Gospel of Christ will face a strict Judgement.

Galatians 5:10 I have confidence in you through the Lord, that ye will be none otherwise minded: but **he that troubleth you shall bear his judgment,** whosoever he be.

We've been made free in Jesus. We're not slaves to our flesh and our performance in keeping the law. This freedom enables us to live holy and to have a loving relationship with God. We are not to use this freedom to satisfy our flesh.

Galatians 5:13 For, brethren, **ye have been called unto liberty; only use not liberty for an occasion to the flesh**, but by love serve one another.

When you trust in your flesh, you're wearing a marred garment.

Jude:23 And others save with fear, pulling them out of the fire; **hating even the garment spotted by the flesh.**

Christ is soon to return to this earth and when He does you must be clothed in His Perfect Righteousness. Destruction awaits those who wear their own garments and have not been clothed by the Lord.

Matthew 22:11 And when the king came in to see the guests, he saw there a man which **had not on a wedding garment**:

Matthew 22:12 And he saith unto him, Friend, how camest thou in hither not having a wedding garment? And he was speechless.

Matthew 22:13 Then said the king to the servants, **Bind him hand and foot, and take him away, and cast him into outer darkness**, there shall be weeping and gnashing of teeth.

When you trust alone in the blood of Jesus, He gives you a white robe.

> Revelation 7:13 And one of the elders answered, saying unto me, **What are these which are arrayed in white robes**? and whence came they?
>
> Revelation 7:14 And I said unto him, Sir, thou knowest. And he said to me, These are they which came out of great tribulation, and **have washed their robes, and made them white in the blood of the Lamb.**

I believe these robes will look like the robe Jesus wore when He was glorified on the mountain (seen by Peter, James & John).

> Mark 9:3 And **his raiment became shining, exceeding white as snow;** so as no fuller on earth can white them.

You must not wear a garment of different sorts. Your robe must be washed white in the blood of Jesus. Don't wear a garment made of a mixture of Jesus's righteousness and your own. Your righteousness is a filthy rag. Don't wear a garment that's been spotted by the flesh.

> Revelation 3:4Thou hast a few names even in Sardis which have not **defiled their garments; and they shall walk with me in white**: for they are worthy.

Are you trusting alone in Jesus? Trust only in Jesus and let your robe be always white.

> Ecclesiastes 9:8 **Let thy garments be always white**; and let thy head lack no ointment.

# Repentance from Dead Works

Grace is an unmerited favor. Another way of saying it would be an undeserved gift. Grace by definition, must be unearned. Once works or merit of any kind are introduced, whatever is received is no longer Grace. That is why Paul says that if Salvation is of works it is no longer grace.

Romans 11:6 And if by grace, then is it no more of works: **otherwise grace is no more grace. But if it be of works, then it is no more grace**: otherwise work is no more work.

To be saved you must accept Salvation as God offers it, which is completely by Grace apart from works.

**Ephesians 2:8 For by grace are ye saved through faith; and that not of yourselves: it is the gift of God:**

**Ephesians 2:9 Not of works, lest any man should boast.**

It is extremely important for you to understand that God requires a special Repentance before you can be saved. You may have heard Repent of Sins in order to be saved, but that's not entirely accurate. You see, to Repent from something is a complete change of mind or turn in direction. God doesn't require you to overcome all your sins before He saves you. As a matter of fact, you won't be able to overcome much at all until you are saved. However, He does require you to Repent of Pride and of all your Dead Works. The very foundation of true Salvation is built upon Repentance from Dead Works.

---

Hebrews 6:6 Therefore leaving the principles of the doctrine of Christ, let us go on unto perfection; **not laying again the foundation of repentance from dead works, and of faith toward God**,

---

What is a dead work you may ask? A Dead Work is any work that is done by a dead person. You see, until you are born again God considers you dead even though your flesh is still alive.

---

| 2 Corinthians 5:14 For the love of Christ constraineth us; because we thus judge, that if one died for all, **then were all dead**: | Matthew 8:22 But Jesus said unto him, Follow me; and **let the dead bury their dead.** |

---

Because we are sinners, we are already dead spiritually until we are born again.

---

Ephesians 2:1 And you hath he quickened, **who were dead in trespasses and sins;**

---

In Leviticus, God says that if a person keeps all His statutes and judgements that they will live in them. In other words, you could have life by following all God's laws. If you never sinned, God would accept you and you would have eternal life.

> Leviticus 18:5 Ye shall therefore keep my statutes, and my judgments: **which if a man do, he shall live in them**: I am the LORD.

He says this again in Ezekiel.

> Ezekiel 20:11 And I gave them my statutes, and shewed them my judgments, **which if a man do, he shall even live in them**.

Living by the Flesh is trusting that what you do in your flesh is what gives you life. It's a trust and a reliance on your works to get you to heaven. God wants you to follow all His laws, but the problem is you can't do it. The person who relies on their works to save them or to keep them saved is not living by faith.

> Galatians 3:12 And **the law is not of faith**: but, The man **that doeth them shall live in them.**

Paul tells us in Romans that Moses described the righteousness of the law and told us that when we lived up to its standards, we would live by it.

> Romans 10:5 For Moses describeth the righteousness which is of the law, That **the man which doeth those things shall live by them**.

If your trust and hope for finding life is in your flesh, the Bible says that you will die. This is what it means to live by the flesh or after the flesh.

Romans 8:13 **For if ye live after the flesh, ye shall die**: but <u>if ye through the Spirit do mortify the deeds of the body, ye shall live.</u>

God wants you to mortify your flesh. To mortify your flesh means you consider it dead. My uncle once went parasailing with one of the straps of his harness connecting him to the parachute nearly cut into (he didn't see it until he was in the air). Someone once asked him if he was scared when he realized it was cut and he replied, "I was mortified!" He was saying that he thought he was a goner or in other words, he considered he was a dead man. This is what you must do and a requirement for being saved. You must realize that you're dead in your flesh and stop trusting in your works to save you.

Romans 6:7 For **he that is dead is freed from sin**.

Romans 6:8 Now **if we be dead with Christ, we believe that we shall also live with him:**

Living by the flesh is not the same thing as fulfilling the lust of the flesh. A natural part of our flesh is to lust after things that could lead us to commit sin. As Christians, we shouldn't fulfill the lust of the flesh, although at times we still do since we are still in a body of flesh. However, we don't find our life in our flesh; we find life in the Spirit by trusting in Jesus and having His Spirit inside of us.

> Romans 8:2 For **the law of the Spirit of life in Christ Jesus hath made me free from the law of sin and death.**
>
> Romans 8:9 But **ye are not in the flesh, but in the Spirit, if so be that the Spirit of God dwell in you**. Now if any man have not the Spirit of Christ, he is none of his.

If we've been made alive by Jesus and His Spirit, we should walk in Him.

> Galatians 5:25 If we live in the Spirit, **let us also walk in the Spirit.**

Walking in the Spirit is a daily walk of faith trusting in Him and focusing on the things of God rather than the things of the world, or as Romans defines it, being spiritually minded. This is where we find peace and where the fruits of the spirit can flow out of us.

> Romans 8:5 For they that are after the flesh do **mind the things of the flesh**; but they that are after the Spirit the things of the Spirit.
>
> Romans 8:6 For to be carnally minded is death; **but to be spiritually minded is life and peace.**

If we walk in the Spirit and keep our focus on the Lord, we won't fulfill the lust of the flesh.

> Galatians 5:16 This I say then, **Walk in the Spirit, and ye shall not fulfil the lust of the flesh.**

The Lord only is Savior. If we participated in accomplishing our Salvation in any way whatsoever it would take away from His Glory. When it comes to Salvation, our only part to play is to watch and to trust. When God brought the Hebrews out of Egypt, He told them to stand still and watch, and that He would fight for them and show them His Salvation.

> Exodus 14:13 And Moses said unto the people, Fear ye not, **stand still, and see the salvation of the LORD**, which he will shew to you to day: for the Egyptians whom ye have seen to day, ye shall see them again no more for ever.
>
> Exodus 14:14 **The LORD shall fight for you, and ye shall hold your peace.**

Remember in Joshua, when the priest shouted, and Jericho fell? You see, it's always the Lord who fights for us and wins our battles. The Lord wants to win the battle of sin and death for you, but in order for that to happen you must surrender your pride.

> Joshua 23:3 And ye have seen all that the LORD your God hath done unto all these nations because of you; for **the LORD your God is he that hath fought for you.**

When flesh is involved in anything good, flesh will always take part in the credit. That's why all throughout the Bible God makes sure everyone knows that Salvation is totally through Him and will not let anyone think they had anything to do with it. That's why He told Gideon to attack the Midianites with a small group of people.

God wanted Gideon and the people to know that it was He who won the battle for them.

> Judges 7:2 And the LORD said unto Gideon, **The people that are with thee are too many** for me to give the Midianites into their hands, **lest Israel vaunt themselves** against me, **saying, Mine own hand hath saved me.**

David understood that the battle against Goliath could only be won by The Lord. We must understand just as David did, that our battle against sin and death can only be won by Jesus.

> 1 Samuel 17:47 And all this assembly shall know that the LORD saveth not with sword and spear: **for the battle is the LORD's**, and he will give you into our hands.

If anyone had a right to trust in their flesh it was the Apostle Paul. You see, before Paul became a Christian, he lived a life following the law and he was blameless according to the law! Blameless is not the same thing as sinless. To be blameless means there is nothing you can be blamed for. In other words, there was nothing you would have seen in Paul's life that you could have found fault with as far as breaking the law.

> Philippians 3:4 Though I might also have confidence in the flesh. **If any other man thinketh that he hath whereof he might trust in the flesh, I more:**
>
> Philippians 3:5 Circumcised the eighth day, of the stock of Israel, of the tribe of Benjamin, an Hebrew of the Hebrews; as touching the law, a Pharisee;
>
> Philippians 3:6 Concerning zeal, persecuting the church; **touching the righteousness which is in the law, blameless.**

However, in other verses Paul admits to being a sinner and to coveting. You see, people usually can't see when we covet or think wrong things in our hearts unless we vocalize our desires, but they are nonetheless sins and put us under the judgment of God. Paul realized this and when he became a Christian, he understood that all his religion was of no benefit when it came to saving him, and he gave it all up for Christ.

> Philippians 3:7 But what **things were gain to me, those I counted loss for Christ.**
>
> Philippians 3:8 Yea doubtless, and I count all things but loss for the excellency of the knowledge of Christ Jesus my Lord: for whom I have suffered the loss of all things, and **do count them but dung, that I may win Christ,**

In Jeremiah, we see that a man is cursed when he puts his trust in man and makes flesh his arm. The arm in scripture symbolizes a man's strength and power to accomplish a task. So, to make flesh your arm is to give power to the flesh to save you.

When you do this, you're departing from the Lord because He only has the power to save, and He only should you put any trust in.

> Jeremiah 17:5 Thus saith the LORD; **Cursed be the man that trusteth in man, and maketh flesh his arm**, and whose heart departeth from the LORD.
>
> Jeremiah 17:7 **Blessed is the man that trusteth in the LORD**, and whose hope the LORD is.

The writer of Hebrews shows us that the sacrifice of Christ should purge our conscience from Dead Works. This is because if we could do anything in our flesh to please God then there would have been no need for Christ to die.

> Hebrews 9:14 How much more shall the blood of Christ, who through the eternal Spirit offered himself without spot to God, **purge your conscience from dead works to serve the living God?**

It's only when we repent of Dead Works that we can serve God in Spirit and in Truth.

> John 4:23 But the hour cometh, and now is, **when the true worshippers shall worship the Father in spirit and in truth**: for the Father seeketh such to worship him.

The Bible is clear about faith apart from works as a means for salvation. However, the critic of salvation by grace apart from works may tell you that turning from sin is not a work. Again, I'm not telling you that as Christians we shouldn't turn from sin.

What I'm telling you is we do this because we are saved and through the power of the Spirit in us, and not as a means of gaining salvation in any way. It's crucial you understand and make this distinction. If you're a drug addict and you turn from that addiction, that in fact is a work. In the book of Jonah, God tells us that when the Ninevites turned from their evil ways it was a work.

Jonah 3:10 **And God saw their <u>works</u>, that they turned from their evil way;** and God repented of the evil, that he had said that he would do unto them; and he did it not.

In the Gospel of John, we read where Jesus was asked what we should do in order to "work the works of God". Jesus tells them that the work that they are to perform is to put their trust in Him. Trusting in Jesus is not a work, but He wanted them, and He wants you to know that what God requires of you is to trust in Jesus, and He will not accept any other work you offer in order to attain salvation.

| John 6:28 Then said they unto him, **What shall we do, that we might work the works of God?** | John 6:29 Jesus answered and said unto them, **This is the work of God, that ye believe on him whom he hath sent.** |
|---|---|

It's not because of our good works that the Lord saves us and lets us into Heaven. It's all by His mercy and grace. He wants to wash you and give you a new life. He will regenerate and renew you if you will lay down your pride.

> Titus 3:5 **Not by works of righteousness which we have done, but according to his mercy he saved us**, by the washing of regeneration, and renewing of the Holy Ghost;

It's better to trust in the Lord than to trust in yourself.

> Psalm 118:8 It is better to trust in the LORD than to put confidence in man.

There are only two types of Religions in the World, which are salvation by works or salvation by grace. Every Religion in the world other than true Christianity is a religion of works. They all have different views as far as how much and what type of righteousness is required, but they all work the same. The Muslim gets to Heaven (in their view) by meeting a certain standard of righteousness as well as the Jew. The Buddhist and Hindu meet a certain standard of righteousness in order to achieve nirvana. The new age believer thinks they will achieve a higher existence by performing good works. True Christianity is the only religion that believes in grace through faith and that our salvation is accomplished strictly by another.

The way to true salvation is narrow.

> Matthew 7:14 Because strait is the gate, and **narrow is the way**, which leadeth unto life, and few there be that find it.

Jesus tells us what the way is. Jesus is the Way. If you're trying to get salvation going any other way than through Jesus, you won't find it.

> John 14:6 Jesus saith unto him, **I am the way**, the truth, and the life: no man cometh unto the Father, but by me.

Habakkuk told us that the just, those declared to be right or righteous, lives by their faith.

> Habakkuk 2:4 Behold, his soul which is lifted up is not upright in him: but **the just shall live by his faith**.

Trying to obey the law will never make you right or justify you before God. If you want to live forever, you must trust alone in Jesus.

> Galatians 3:11 But that **no man is justified by the law in the sight of God**, it is evident: for, **The just shall live by faith**.

This is what God revealed to the prophets, that the Just would find life through faith, and this faith is in Jesus!

> Romans 1:17 For therein is the righteousness of God revealed from faith to faith: as it is written, **The just shall live by faith.**

Have you Repented of Dead Works? Have you been made Alive through Faith in Jesus, or are you still living by the Flesh?

# Call Upon the Name of the Lord

Have you ever heard of the term "Call Upon the Name of the Lord"? When I was young, I remember hearing preachers talk about calling upon the name of the Lord. I remember hearing them say that anyone who would call upon the Lord would be saved. Since I didn't fully understand the Gospel at that time, and because I misinterpreted what they said, I thought that to "Call Upon the Lord" was to cry out "Lord Help Me!" and that anyone who did this could find salvation.

There is certainly truth in the fact that if you cry out to the Lord and ask Him to help you, you can find salvation. However, what we learn is that God has shown us in His word what He means by "Call Upon the Name of the Lord" and when we call upon His name it must be after the model that He provides in His word and not a generic calling upon God for help.

We first see people calling upon the Lord in Genesis. The Bible tells us that when Enos was born men began to call upon the name of the Lord. Enos was the grandson of Adam and the son of Seth. Adam, who lived to be 930 years old, was 235 years old when Enos was born.

The Bible doesn't tell us exactly why men began to call upon the Lord at this time. This was after Cain had slew Abel and it's possible that other people may have died either by disease, accident, or murder. We don't know for sure. In my mind, I think there may have been other people who died around this time, children or grandchildren of Adam, that could have prompted this.

> Genesis 4:26 And to Seth, to him also there was born a son; and he called his name Enos: **then began men to call upon the name of the LORD.**

Later, we see Abraham (Abram at the time) built an altar and called upon the name of the Lord.

> Genesis 12:8 And he removed from thence unto a mountain on the east of Bethel, and pitched his tent, having Bethel on the west, and Hai on the east: and there he builded an altar unto the LORD, **and called upon the name of the LORD.**

In Psalm 116, God shows us what it means to call upon the Lord and how we are to call upon Him. There are three parts to calling upon the Lord. Now, no one can call upon the Lord unless the Lord calls them first. God the Father must draw you to Himself and to the Son.

> John 6:44 **No man can come to me, except the Father which hath sent me draw him**: and I will raise him up at the last day.

When the Father starts to draw you, the first thing He will do is show you that you are separated from Him. You will realize that you are in a lost condition. A fear will come upon you, and you will realize that destruction awaits you if you remain in your current state, and that you are going to be held accountable to a Holy God.

> Proverbs 9:10 **The fear of the LORD is the beginning of wisdom**: and the knowledge of the holy is understanding.

If the Father has begun to draw you and has put His fear upon you, you will realize that you are headed to Hell unless you are saved, and no religious acts will make you feel any better, you will have trouble and sorrow.

> Psalm 116:3 The sorrows of death compassed me, and the pains of hell gat hold upon me: I found trouble and sorrow.

When this happens, you Call Upon the Lord and ask Him to deliver you.

> Psalm 116:4 **Then called I upon the name of the LORD**; O LORD, I beseech thee, deliver my soul.

You may ask what is the Name of the Lord? This is a good question, and it is asked in Proverbs.

> Proverbs 30:4 Who hath ascended up into heaven, or descended? who hath gathered the wind in his fists? who hath bound the waters in a garment? who hath established all the ends of the earth? **what is his name, and what is his son's name, if thou canst tell?**

In order to Call Upon the Name of the Lord, someone does in fact need to explain to you who the Lord is.

Romans 10:14 **How then shall they call on him** in whom they have not believed? **and how shall they believe in him of whom they have not heard**? and how shall they hear without a preacher?

There is only one Name to Call Upon for Salvation.

Acts 4:12 Neither is there salvation in any other: **for there is none other name under heaven given among men, whereby we must be saved.**

The Name of the Lord is Jesus! His name is above every other name, and at His name shall every knee bow and confess that He is Lord!

Philippians 2:9 Wherefore God also hath highly exalted him, and given him **a name which is above every name**:
Philippians 2:10 That **at the name of Jesus every knee should bow**, of things in heaven, and things in earth, and things under the earth;
Philippians 2:11 And that **every tongue should confess that Jesus Christ is Lord**, to the glory of God the Father.

Now that you know the Name of the Lord that you are to call upon let's get back to Psalm 116. When you call upon the Lord for help, He has something to offer you. You see, God won't just forgive your sin. Because God is Just, He must punish your sin. However, He offers you a gift which He refers to as the cup of salvation. You must take this cup if you want to be saved.

> Psalm 116:13 <u>I will take the cup of salvation</u>, **and call upon the name of the LORD.**

The cup of salvation that you must drink is the blood of Jesus. It's the blood that Jesus shed on your behalf to save you.

> Matthew 26:27 And **he took the cup**, and gave thanks, and gave it to them, saying, Drink ye all of it;
>
> Matthew 26:28 For **this is my blood of the new testament, which is shed for many for the remission of sins.**

Whoever drinks this blood will live forever.

> John 6:54 Whoso eateth my flesh, **and drinketh my blood, hath eternal life**; and I will raise him up at the last day.

You must understand how to drink the blood of Jesus. In John 6, Jesus compares physical food and drink to spiritual food and drink. He explains how physical food and drink give temporary life while His body and blood give eternal life. You see, our bodies require food and water to survive. We can live longer without food than water. Without water, we won't live very long. What God wants is for you to consider that it's the blood of Jesus that gives you life. It's His life and death on the cross that allows you to have eternal life. To eat His flesh and drink His blood is to put your trust in Him and believe that it's what He accomplished with His life and death that is getting you to Heaven. Don't trust in your religious practices, but completely trust in what He accomplished with His life and death.

> Luke 22:19 And **he took bread**, and gave thanks, and brake it, and gave unto them, saying, **This is my body which is given for you**: this do in remembrance of me.
>
> Luke 22:20 Likewise **also the cup** after supper, saying, **This cup is the new testament in my blood, which is shed for you.**

If you've drank the cup of salvation, you have received God's grace and mercy. It is only by grace and mercy that we are saved. Grace is an undeserved gift and mercy is an undeserved pardon. God's grace lets us live forever in His presence and His mercy keeps us out of Hell.

> Psalm 116:5 Gracious is the LORD, and righteous; yea, our God is merciful.

Also, when you have received forgiveness and you realize that your soul has been saved from death it will bring you peace and rest.

> Psalm 116:7 **Return unto thy rest, O my soul**; for the LORD hath dealt bountifully with thee.
> Psalm 116:8 **For thou hast delivered my soul from death**, mine eyes from tears, and my feet from falling

The last part of Calling Upon the Lord is the sacrifice of thanksgiving. This is a sacrifice we offer to the Lord because we are thankful for His Salvation and what He has done for us.

> Psalm 116:7 I will offer to thee the sacrifice of thanksgiving, **and will call upon the name of the LORD.**
>
> 1 Chronicles 16:8 **Give thanks unto the LORD, call upon his name**, make known his deeds among the people.

As Christians, there are different types of spiritual sacrifices we are to offer God.

> 1 Peter 2:5 Ye also, as lively stones, are built up a spiritual house, an holy priesthood, **to offer up spiritual sacrifices**, acceptable to God by Jesus Christ.

One type of sacrifice we should offer God is the sacrifice of righteousness. This is where we should live a life that is pleasing and acceptable to Him.

> Psalm 4: **Offer the sacrifices of righteousness**, and put your trust in the LORD.

We should also offer the sacrifice of praise. This is where we give Him thanks for everything in our lives.

> Hebrews 13:15 By him therefore **let us offer the sacrifice of praise** to God continually, that is, the fruit of our lips **giving thanks to his name.**

As a Christian, we don't offer these sacrifices in order that we would be saved or that we might maintain our salvation. If you're doing this, you're not drinking the cup of salvation. We offer these sacrifices because we understand what God has done for us. We ask ourselves the question David asked, which is, what can we do for God because of what He has done for me?

> Psalm 116:12 What shall I render unto the LORD for all his benefits toward me?

Another way we honor God and praise Him is by being among His people. Christians should assemble and support each other.

> Psalm 116:14 I will pay my vows unto the LORD now in the presence of all his people.

The Bible shows us this is important and that we shouldn't forsake it.

> Hebrews 10:25 **Not forsaking the assembling of ourselves together**, as the manner of some is; but exhorting one another: and so much the more, as ye see the day approaching.

Joel prophesied of a day coming when the Lord would pour out His Spirit and that whoever called upon the name of the Lord would be saved.

> Joel 2: **And it shall come to pass, that whosoever shall call on the name of the LORD shall be delivered**: for in mount Zion and in Jerusalem shall be deliverance, as the LORD hath said, and in the remnant whom the LORD shall call.

Peter told us that to Call Upon the Lord is to Call Upon and to put your trust in Jesus.

> Acts 2:21 And it shall come to pass, that **whosoever shall call on the name of the Lord shall be saved.**
>
> Acts 2:36 Therefore let all the house of Israel know assuredly, that **God hath made the same Jesus**, whom ye have crucified, **both Lord and Christ.**

Paul told us that the Lord is rich unto all that call upon Him. That means He has plenty of Grace and Mercy that He wants to give you.

Romans 10:12 For there is no difference between the Jew and the Greek: for **the same Lord over all is rich unto all that call upon him**.

Romans 10:13 For **whosoever shall call upon the name of the Lord shall be saved.**

Jeremiah called upon the Lord when he needed help. He found that when you call upon the Lord with a pure heart the Lord hears and offers help and redemption.

Lamentations 3:55 **I called upon thy name, O LORD**, out of the low dungeon.
Lamentations 3:56 **Thou hast heard my voice**: hide not thine ear at my breathing, at my cry.
Lamentations 3:57 Thou drewest near in the day that I called upon thee: thou saidst, **Fear not**.
Lamentations 3:58 O LORD, thou hast pleaded the causes of my soul; **thou hast redeemed my life.**

There is a day coming when all who have Called Upon the Lord will serve Him in unison.

Zephaniah 3:9 For then will I turn to the people a pure language, that **they may all call upon the name of the LORD, to serve him with one consent.**

Jesus conquered our enemies, Satan, Death, and all Darkness. Our job is to sit at the table He has prepared and to drink the Cup He offers.

---

Psalm 23:5 <u>Thou preparest a table before me in the presence of mine enemies</u>: thou anointest my head with oil; **my cup runneth over**.

Matthew 26:27 And he took the cup, and gave thanks, and gave it to them, saying, **<u>Drink ye all of it;</u>**

---

The cup is full and spilling over the top, and you must drink the entire cup. That means you trust totally in the Blood of Jesus for your Salvation! Are you among those who have Called Upon the Lord? Have you Called Upon Jesus?

# You Must Be Born Again

What do you think of when you hear the term "Christian"? To many, a Christian is someone who has conservative values, goes to church, and admits that Jesus died for sinners. Technically, a Christian is someone who follows Jesus. There's another class of Christian (speaking from the view of the world) called Born Again Christians. To the World, Born Again Christians are a class that's a little more serious about their faith and usually a little stricter. They are a class that claims to have had an experience and are not just mentally agreeing to the claim that Jesus is Lord.

The truth is, if you're a real Christian you have been Born Again. Unless you are Born Again, you are not saved even though you may have been through some type of ritual such as water baptism, walking an aisle, or raising your hand when a preacher asked, etc. Jesus told Nicodemus (A Pharisee) that unless a person is Born Again, they would not see the Kingdom of God.

John 3:3 Jesus answered and said unto him, Verily, verily, I say unto thee, **Except a man be born again, he cannot see the kingdom of God**.

Jesus went on to explain that for a person to be in God's Kingdom they would have to have had a spiritual birth. The water in verse 5 is not water baptism (as some claim) but is rather the Water of the Spirit.

John 3:5 Jesus answered, Verily, verily, I say unto thee, <u>Except a man be born of water and of the Spirit</u>, he cannot enter into the kingdom of God.

John 3:6 **That which is born of the flesh is flesh**; and **that which is born of the Spirit is spirit.**

John 3:7 Marvel not that I said unto thee, **Ye must be born again.**

The New Testament compares the Holy Spirit with water in many places. The Water of the Holy Spirit gives us life. The Water also cleanses us.

Ephesians 5:26 That he might sanctify and cleanse it with the washing of water by the word,

The "washing of water by the Word", spoken of in Ephesians, refers to the "Washing of Regeneration". This is the regeneration of our spirits which takes place when we are born of the Spirit of God. It is the Holy Ghost, which is God's Spirit that comes inside of us, that does this washing and renews us.

Titus 3:5 Not by works of righteousness which we have done, but according to his mercy he saved us, **by the washing of regeneration, and renewing of the Holy Ghost;**

The Water, which is also the Spirit, flows forth from Jesus. He is the Well and the Fountain. That's why Jesus offered the Water to the woman at the well in Samaria. He was telling her that He could offer her the Holy Spirit. He also told her the Water would become a well within her that would spring up into Everlasting Life. In other words, if she drank of the Water, she would have Eternal Life and the Water would remain within her!

John 4:10 Jesus answered and said unto her, If thou knewest the gift of God, and who it is that saith to thee, Give me to drink; thou wouldest have asked of him, and **he would have given thee living water.**

John 4:14 **But whosoever drinketh of the water that I shall give him shall never thirst; but the water that I shall give him shall be in him a well of water springing up into everlasting life.**

To be born again you must understand that you are dead in your sins. When the Hebrews came out of Egypt, they encountered some deadly snakes that were biting them and killing them. God told Moses to make a bronze serpent and put it on a pole, and to tell the people who were bit to look upon it. When they looked upon it, they would be healed. They were to behold the thing that was killing them lifted up on a pole.

Numbers 21:8 And the LORD said unto Moses, Make thee a fiery serpent, and set it upon a pole: and it shall come to pass, that every one that is bitten, **when he looketh upon it, shall live.**

In the same manner, we are to behold Jesus lifted up on the cross and realize that He became sin for us, that is, He became the sinner in place of us, because we are sinners and deserve to die. When you see Jesus on the cross, realize that is supposed to be you and realize that your sin has killed you. Because Jesus died for you and took your place, He now offers you a new life.

John 3:14 And **as Moses lifted up the serpent in the wilderness**, even so must the Son of man be lifted up:

John 3:15 That whosoever believeth in him should not perish, but have eternal life.

I tell you that Jesus offers you a new life. Salvation is a Free Gift. Salvation also comes as a package deal. What I mean by that is, God doesn't save you and then leave you alone while you live the rest of your life. He doesn't give you a ticket to Heaven that you hide away, and then you go live the rest of your life until it comes time to turn your ticket in. Salvation is not fire insurance against hell. To be Born Again is to be a new creation. If you've been Born Again, you're not the same person as you once were.

> 2 Corinthians 5:17 **Therefore if any man be in Christ, he is a new creature:** old things are passed away; behold, all things are become new.

There is a cost to this Salvation and Jesus tells us we need to count the cost (Luke 14: 28-30). When Jesus saves you and you are Born Again you will become a new creature. The way you view the world and other people will change, and the way you view sin will change.

One of the things the Lord wants you to consider is that becoming a Christian could cause you to lose your earthly family. While this may not be too common in the Western world, it's very common for Muslims and Jews to be kicked out of the family for becoming a Christian. If you choose to maintain a relationship with your earthly family over having a relationship with God, you won't be saved. No true Christian will accuse the Lord of coming between them and their family when they stand before Him, because they will have willingly chosen Him over their family.

> Matthew 10:35 For I am come to set a man at variance against his father, and the daughter against her mother, and the daughter in law against her mother in law.
>
> Matthew 10:36 And a man's foes shall be they of his own household.
>
> Matthew 10:37 **He that loveth father or mother more than me is not worthy of me: and he that loveth son or daughter more than me is not worthy of me.**

You must also understand that as a result of being Born Again, your life will change. This isn't the result of becoming more religious once you're Born Again, but it's the result of the Holy Spirit living within you and sanctifying you. Also, because you will now be in a relationship with God again, He is going to chastise you when you sin. Among other things, this means you cannot live a life of selfishness or wickedness without your soul being grieved. If you try to live a life focused on money and things, you will be chastised by God if you're a true Born-Again Believer.

Jesus wants you to understand this, and so He also wants you to be willing to give up the life you have now in place of the new life He offers you. If you want to hold on to the life you have now and just live for yourself, you won't be saved. God changes people when they are Born Again, but He isn't going to change you against your will. You must take up your cross and follow Jesus. To take up your cross means you realize you are going to your death. Anytime someone was seen carrying a cross everyone knew what was going to happen. That person was on their way to their death, to be crucified.

You must be willing to let your current life go and accept the new life Jesus offers. This is a life of joy and peace, and I promise you no one who has ever been truly Born Again would trade their old life for the new one.

Matthew 10:38 And he that taketh not his cross, and followeth after me, is not worthy of me.

Matthew 10:39 **He that findeth his life shall lose it: and he that loseth his life for my sake shall find it.**

If you understand that you are dead in your sins and you understand that Salvation is a new life in relationship with God, all God requires of you is to put your trust in Him through Faith in Jesus, Faith in the Gospel. There is no other work God requires of you to be Born Again. Realize you're a sinner who can't save themselves. Realize Jesus is God in flesh who died in your place for your sins, and that He was buried and rose again to Justify you. Place all your trust in Jesus and the Gospel. If you truly understand Salvation and what is offered to you, and you place all your trust in Jesus, you will be Saved and Sealed by God's Holy Spirit.

Ephesians 1:12 That we should be to the praise of his glory, **who first trusted in Christ.**

Ephesians 1:13 **In whom ye also <u>trusted</u>, after that ye heard the word of truth, <u>the gospel of your salvation</u>**: in whom also after that ye believed, **ye were sealed with that holy Spirit of promise,**

Never let a Wolf tell you that more is required to be Born Again and to be Saved than Trusting in Jesus. Satan wants to move your trust in Jesus to trusting in yourself and your works. Many will come to Jesus at the end and find they are rejected because they did not do the Will of the Father.

> Matthew 7: Not every one that saith unto me, Lord, Lord, shall enter into the kingdom of heaven; **but he that doeth the will of my Father which is in heaven.**
>
> Matthew 12:50 For **whosoever shall do the will of my Father** which is in heaven, the same is my brother, and sister, and mother.

It's important you understand what the Will of the Father for you is. You see, it's God's Perfect Will for us to be perfectly sinless, but because He knows we can't achieve that, He sent Jesus. Jesus came down from Heaven and fulfilled the Will of the Father perfectly. Jesus lived a perfect life, did everything the Father commanded, and died on the cross for our sins. By doing so, He fulfilled the Will of the Father.

> John 6:38 For I came down from heaven, not to do mine own will, but **the will of him that sent me.**

In addition to fulfilling God's Will on earth by living as the Perfect Man and becoming our Sacrifice, Jesus tells us it is also the Will of the Father that He keeps those who the Father gives Him, and that He raises them up on the last day!

> John 6:39 And **this is the Father's will which hath sent me,** that of all which he hath given me **I should lose nothing,** but should raise it up again at the last day.

Then, Jesus tells us what our part is in keeping the Father's Will. The part we play and the way in which we keep the Father's Will is, we believe on Jesus, which means we put our Trust in Him!

> John 6:40 And **this is the will of him that sent me,** that every one which **seeth the Son, and believeth on him, may have everlasting life**: and I will raise him up at the last day.

Many will come to Jesus at the end and will be cast away because they fell into Satan's trap and into a false gospel. They trusted it was their good works that saved them and/or kept them saved. Notice, they don't say "Lord didn't we trust you died for our sins". Their trust is in their works. To be Born Again you must trust alone in Jesus.

> Matthew 7:22 Many will say to me in that day, Lord, Lord, have we not prophesied in thy name? and in thy name have cast out devils? and **in thy name done many wonderful works**?

The Bible describes saving belief as Trust. It's one thing to believe in your mind, or mentally agree to the fact that Jesus died for us. It's a different thing to Trust in the Lord with all your heart and to trust totally that what He did was sufficient to save you. One way the Bible describes Trusting the Lord is like chicks who abide under the wings of their mother, who shelters and protects them from all things.

Psalm 17:8 Keep me as the apple of the eye, **hide me under the shadow of thy wings,**
Psalm 36:7 How excellent is thy lovingkindness, O God! therefore the children of men put their **trust under the shadow of thy wings.**
Psalm 57:1 Be merciful unto me, O God, be merciful unto me: **for my soul trusteth in thee**: yea, **in the shadow of thy wings will I make my refuge,** until these calamities be overpast.
Psalm 91:4 He shall cover thee with his feathers, **and under his wings shalt thou trust**: his truth shall be thy shield and buckler.

When Jesus was on earth, most of the Jews rejected Him and didn't put their trust in Him.

Matthew 23:37 O Jerusalem, Jerusalem, thou that killest the prophets, and stonest them which are sent unto thee, **how often would I have gathered thy children together, even as a hen gathereth her chickens under her wings**, and ye would not!

In contrast, Ruth who was a Gentile, and a Moabite woman, found grace by Trusting in the Lord.  Ruth was the great grandmother of King David.

Ruth 2:12 The LORD recompense thy work, and a full reward be given thee of the LORD God of Israel, **under whose wings thou art come to trust.**

When Jesus was on earth, He kept all the Commandments in the Law.  He kept the 10 plus the other 600+.

John 15:10 If ye keep my commandments, ye shall abide in my love; even as **I have kept my Father's commandments**, and abide in his love.

We should honor God's law. It is holy and righteous. However, it's important that you understand and are clear about the fact that you can't keep it. As a Christian, you do have Commandments to keep though. First and foremost, your commandment is to Trust in Jesus. Secondly, we are to love each other. The second can only be kept after you've been Born Again, and the Holy Spirit gives you the power to love the way He wants you to.

1 John 3:23 **And this is his commandment**, That we should **believe on the name of his Son Jesus Christ, and love one another**, as he gave us commandment.

When you Trust in Jesus and His Gospel, and are truly Born Again, the Holy Spirit will live inside of you. Don't let anyone tell you that you are saved. It is the Holy Spirit and Him alone that you should trust to give you confirmation that you've been Born Again.

1 John 3:24 And he that keepeth his commandments dwelleth in him, and he in him. And **hereby we know that he abideth in us, by the Spirit which he hath given us.**

If you've been saved, the Holy Spirit will bear witness with your spirit. That means God will give you a confirmation in your heart that you belong to Him.

Romans 8:16 **The Spirit itself beareth witness with our spirit**, that we are the children of God:

If you don't have this witness within yourself, the answer is not to try to be better. You must make sure you understand the Gospel and make sure that you want to have a relationship with the Lord. The more you Trust that what Jesus did is enough to save you, the more peace you will have.

Isaiah 26:3 **Thou wilt keep him in perfect peace**, whose mind is stayed on thee: **because he trusteth in thee**.

Trust in Jesus with all your heart. Don't think you have to have all the answers to everything, just believe what Jesus did is enough to save you.

Proverbs 3: **Trust in the LORD with all thine heart**; and lean not unto thine own understanding.

When you know that you have been Born Again you will have a peace within you that is unexplainable.

Philippians 4:7 And **the peace of God, which passeth all understanding**, shall keep your hearts and minds through Christ Jesus.

In the end, the most important thing is that you've been Born Again. It's not your church attendance, tithing, giving to the poor, abstaining from drugs or alcohol (all good and wise things to do) that gets you to Heaven. God doesn't save us because of our works or keep us saved because of our works.

> 2 Timothy 1: **Who hath saved us**, and called us with an holy calling, **not according to our works,** but according to his own purpose and grace, which was given us in Christ Jesus before the world began,

Remember, what matters is that you've been Born Again and are a new creature, a new creation in Christ.

> Galatians 6:15 For in Christ Jesus neither circumcision availeth any thing, nor uncircumcision, **but a new creature**.

Have you been made a new creature? Do you know that you've been Born Again?

# One Lord, One Faith, One Baptism

What do you think of when you hear the word "Baptism"? For many, baptism means being immersed in water. While it's true water baptism is a common type of baptism, there are other baptisms both in common everyday life and in the Bible. It's important that you understand what Baptism is, because if you're confused, it can cause problems when trying to interpret what the Bible says about salvation. Now, baptism is an immersion whereby the thing that is immersed is then identified with the thing it is immersed into.

There is one Baptism in the Bible that is essential for salvation. However, contrary to the beliefs of certain Christian Denominations, it is not water baptism. Did you know that the New Testament talks about 7 different baptisms? The book of Hebrews also tells us that there is a doctrine of baptisms. I think it's important for any Christian who wants to understand their Bible and get closer to the Lord, to understand this doctrine.

Hebrews 6:2 **Of the doctrine of baptisms**, and of laying on of hands, and of resurrection of the dead, and of eternal judgment.

We're going to take a look at the 7 Baptisms in this chapter. The purpose of this chapter is not to minimalize the importance of water baptism. I will tell you now that if you are a true Christian, you should be water-baptized. If you refuse to be water baptized that could indicate a problem, which we'll talk more about. However, for the sake of understanding the Gospel and trusting alone in Jesus, we need to understand the role water baptism plays (it doesn't save you). We'll also show which baptism is required for salvation. Each of the 7 Baptisms will contain 3 elements which are- the baptizer, the person being baptized, and the substance the person is being baptized into.

The First Baptism is the <u>Baptism of Repentance.</u> This baptism was performed by John the Baptist. When a person repented of trusting in works for their salvation, and trusted alone in Christ, they were eligible to receive the Baptism of Repentance. The baptizer for this baptism was John the Baptist, and the substance the person was immersed into was water.

Acts 19:4 Then said Paul, **John verily baptized with the baptism of repentance**, <u>saying unto the people, that they should believe on him which should come after him, that is, on Christ Jesus</u>.

Both forms of water baptism that we are going to look at in this chapter symbolize a couple of things. First, water baptism symbolizes a death and a resurrection. It also represents a cleansing of the flesh.

In the Old Testament, the priests had to wash themselves in water before they could offer the sacrifices.

Exodus 40:12 And thou shalt bring Aaron and his sons unto the door of the tabernacle of the congregation, **and wash them with water**.

When King Solomon built the Temple, he made a tub for the priest to wash in. They called this the "Molten Sea" because it was made from molten brass. It was approximately 15 feet wide, 45 feet in circumference, and 7 ½ feet deep!

2 Chronicles 4:2 Also he made a molten sea of ten cubits from brim to brim, round in compass, and five cubits the height thereof; and a line of thirty cubits did compass it round about.

Jesus was baptized by John the Baptist. There are people who will point to this and tell you that this proves water baptism is involved in salvation. Jesus didn't get water baptized in order to wash away sins because He didn't have any! In my opinion, the primary reason Jesus was water baptized was because He was about to begin His ministry and as our Great High Priest, He was following the pattern of the washing of the priests in the Old Testament. The priests in the Old Testament needed sanctification and to be washed before offering sacrifices to God but Jesus did not! He was fulfilling His Priestly role. I believe Jesus also wanted to identify with His people and set a good example for us to follow. As I stated, water baptism represents death and resurrection. It also represents a cleansing and is related to the washing of the priests in the Old Testament.

When John the Baptist was baptizing, he stated that One was coming after him that was greater than himself, referring to Jesus. He also stated that this One (Jesus) would also baptize, but instead of using water, He would use the Holy Ghost and Fire. In one verse, we see three of the seven baptisms.

> Matthew 3:11 I indeed **baptize you <u>with water</u> unto repentance.** but he that cometh after me is mightier than I, whose shoes I am not worthy to bear: **he shall baptize you <u>with the Holy Ghost</u>, and <u>with fire:</u>**

This brings us to the second baptism we'll look at, which is the <u>Baptism of Fire</u>. Some believe the baptism of fire is an extra powerful dose of the baptism of the Holy Ghost, which we'll look at also, but that is not correct. If you hear anyone say that they are seeking the Baptism of Fire, they misunderstand what they are seeking after. In this baptism, the Baptizer is Jesus. The person who is being baptized is immersed into The Lake of Fire. John the Baptist who is speaking in these verses, explains what the Baptism of Fire is.

> Matthew 3:12 <u>Whose fan is in his hand</u>, and he will throughly purge his floor, and gather his wheat into the garner; but **he will burn up the chaff with unquenchable fire.**

Next, we'll look at the <u>Baptism of Moses</u>. To note, these baptisms as I'm listing them are not in sequential scriptural order, so if I say 1$^{st}$, 2$^{nd}$, 3$^{rd}$, that does not mean this is the sequence they occur in scripture, but rather just the order as I am presenting them.

The Baptism of Moses is not a baptism that we receive today nor that any Christian ever would have received. This baptism is mentioned in the New Testament as a reference to what happened in the past and Paul uses it to make a point.

> 1 Corinthians 10:1 Moreover, brethren, I would not that ye should be ignorant, how that all our fathers were under the cloud, and all passed through the sea;
>
> 1 Corinthians 10:2 **And were all baptized unto Moses** in the cloud and in the sea;

The Person doing the baptizing in the Baptism of Moses is God. The people who are being baptized are the Hebrews who followed Moses out of Egypt. The substance they are being baptized with is Moses. They are being baptized unto Moses which means God is associating them with Moses. Moses was the person who God had a relationship with and dealt with directly. When they followed Moses through the cloud and through the Red Sea, they became baptized unto Moses. In other words, they were fully immersed and associated with Moses in God's eyes.

Next, we'll look at the <u>Baptism of Suffering</u>. Jesus told the disciples about a baptism that He was going to have to endure. He wasn't looking forward to this baptism, but He knew it was necessary.

> Luke 12:50 **But I have a baptism to be baptized with**; and how am I straitened till it be accomplished!

The baptism He was referring to was the suffering that He was about to endure going to the cross. Jesus also told His disciples that they would be baptized with this Baptism of Suffering. Most of the apostles suffered and died horrible deaths. Our Bibles don't tell us how the apostles died, but history says that Peter was crucified upside down and that Paul was beheaded. History also says the other apostles except for maybe John, were martyred. Historians think John was the only apostle (of the 11) who might have died from old age.

> Mark 10:38 But Jesus said unto them, Ye know not what ye ask: can ye drink of the cup that I drink of? and **be baptized with the baptism that I am baptized with?**
>
> Mark 10:39 And they said unto him, We can. And Jesus said unto them, Ye shall indeed drink of the cup that I drink of; **and with the baptism that I am baptized withal shall ye be baptized:**

The baptizer for this baptism would be the people inflicting the suffering on Jesus and the apostles, and the substance they were being immersed into was suffering and death.

Now, we're going to look at the <u>Baptism into Christ</u>. This is the One Baptism that is required for Salvation. There is no water involved in this Baptism. The Person who performs this baptism is the Holy Spirit. The person getting baptized is the believer, and the substance the person is being baptized into is Jesus Christ.

> 1 Corinthians 12:13 **For by one Spirit are we all baptized into one body,** whether we be Jews or Gentiles, whether we be bond or free; and have been all made to drink into one Spirit.

When a person trusts with all their heart in the blood of Jesus, not their works, or trusting in their own righteousness, they are saved. It's with the heart that a person believes in Jesus and becomes accounted righteous. With our heart, we believe and become righteous, and with our mouths, we confess that we are saved.

> Romans 10: For **with the heart man believeth unto righteousness**; and with the mouth confession is made unto salvation.

When this happens, the Holy Spirit baptizes us into Jesus, and we become part of the Body of Christ. That means when Jesus died, we died, when Jesus was buried, we were buried, and when Jesus rose, we rose!

> Romans 6:3 Know ye not, that **so many of us as were baptized into Jesus Christ were baptized into his death**?
>
> Romans 6:4 Therefore **we are buried with him by baptism into death**: that like as Christ was raised up from the dead by the glory of the Father, even so we also should walk in newness of life.
>
> Romans 6:5 For if we have been planted together in the likeness of his death, **we shall be also in the likeness of his resurrection**:
>
> Galatians 3:27 For as many of you **as have been baptized into Christ have put on Christ.**

Like I said, the Baptism into Christ is done by the Holy Spirit when a person believes. It has nothing to do with water. The water comes afterward and is important, but you must not confuse the expression of your salvation with the power of your salvation.

There are a few verses in the Bible that are commonly misunderstood and that some people use to show that water baptism is required for salvation. A couple of these come from 1 Peter Chapter 3.

> 1 Peter 3:20 Which sometime were disobedient, when once the longsuffering of God waited in the days of Noah, while **the ark** was a preparing, **wherein few, that is, eight souls were saved by water.**
>
> 1 Peter 3:21 **The like figure** whereunto even baptism doth also now save us (**not the putting away of the filth of the flesh**, but the answer of a good conscience toward God,) by the resurrection of Jesus Christ:

Some people look at 1 Peter 3:20-21 and see that Noah and his family were <u>saved by water,</u> and so immediately their minds go to water baptism when the next verse uses the word baptism. If you remember the story of Noah, they weren't saved by water but from water. The water that Peter is referring to is not physical water but the Spirit of God. One of the ways the Bible describes the Spirit of God is by calling Him Water. Water is crucial to our survival, and it also cleanses us, but God's Spirit is more important than physical water.

> Ephesians 5:26 That he might sanctify and cleanse it with **the washing of water by the word,**

It was God's Spirit and Word that saved Noah and his family. The place they were saved was the Ark. Noah and his family being in the Ark is a figure of the Christian being in Christ. When we are Baptized into Christ, we are saved from God's Wrath just as Noah was saved from the flood.

This verse can be confusing and that's why Peter specifies that it's "not the putting away of the filth of the flesh" or water baptism that he's referring to. He's referring to being spiritually Baptized into Christ.

Another misunderstood verse is in Mark 16. This verse shows that if a person believes and is baptized, they will be saved, but if they don't believe they'll be damned.

> Mark 16:**16 He that believeth and is baptized shall be saved**; but **he that believeth not shall be damned**.

Notice, he says that he who doesn't believe will be damned. The reason he doesn't say "he who doesn't believe or be baptized will be damned" is because the baptism he's referring to happens simultaneously with saving belief. There will be people who believe in their heads about Jesus and are water baptized that will go to Hell. On the other hand, the people that will be saved are those who truly believed in their heart and who were Baptized into Christ spiritually.

Next, let's look at the Baptism of the Holy Ghost. This is another baptism that is commonly misunderstood. The Baptism of the Holy Ghost is not the same as the Baptism into Christ. The Person doing the baptizing in this baptism is Jesus. The believer is baptized by Jesus and the substance used is the Holy Ghost.

> Acts 1:5 For John truly baptized with water; but **ye shall be baptized with the Holy Ghost** not many days hence.

While the purpose of the Baptism into Christ is to immerse us into Jesus so that His death is our death and His resurrection is our resurrection, the purpose of the Baptism of the Holy Ghost is to immerse us in the Holy Ghost in order to empower us to be The Lord's Witnesses.

> Acts 1:8 But **ye shall receive power, after that the Holy Ghost is come upon you: and ye shall be witnesses unto me** both in Jerusalem, and in all Judaea, and in Samaria, and unto the uttermost part of the earth.

It's important that you understand the difference between being Baptized into Christ and the Baptism of the Holy Ghost. You get Baptized into Christ through faith when you put your Trust in the Gospel of Christ. This happens in your heart. However, the Baptism of the Holy Ghost comes a few different ways. It can come through prayer and praise such as the original 120 in the upper room at Pentecost. It can also come when someone who has already been baptized in the Holy Ghost lays their hands on you.

> Acts 8:17 Then **laid they their hands on them**, and they received the Holy Ghost.
> Acts 19:6 And when Paul had **laid his hands upon them**, the Holy Ghost came on them; and they spake with tongues, and prophesied.

It's a common misunderstanding that the apostles and other disciples were saved on the day of Pentecost. What actually happened on Pentecost is they received the Baptism of the Holy Ghost. They were saved weeks earlier when Jesus rose and appeared to them, and they believed and trusted the Gospel.

When the apostles and original disciples saw Jesus risen and believed upon Him, Jesus breathed on them and breathed the Spirit inside of them.

John 20:22 And when he had said this, **he breathed on them**, and saith unto them, **Receive ye the Holy Ghost**:

Jesus breathed the Spirit of life into them just as He had originally done to Adam in the Garden of Eden. Adam lost his life when he failed to keep God's law (he only had one law, not to eat the forbidden fruit). Unlike Adam, we don't keep our life through the law but by trusting in Jesus who kept the law for us.

Genesis 2:7 And the LORD God formed man of the dust of the ground, **and breathed into his nostrils the breath of life**; and man became a living soul.

Later on the Day of Pentecost, the Holy Ghost came upon them and they received power to be Witnesses. This was the power the apostles would need to show the world that Jesus was God and Savior, which included the ability to speak in tongues, prophesy, perform healings and miracles.

Acts 2:4 And they were all filled with the Holy Ghost, and began to speak with other tongues, as the Spirit gave them utterance.

The Baptism of the Holy Ghost is still available today although few seek after it. The Apostles received a special power and anointing that was not common to the average believer. However, God still wants to give us power today to speak His Word and to be His witnesses.

Lastly, we'll look at <u>Believer's Baptism</u>. This is the baptism we are supposed to participate in after we have trusted in Christ and have been Born Again. This comes after Salvation, not before or in order to achieve Salvation. The baptizer for this baptism is another believer. It's usually done by a pastor or elder in the church, but the Bible doesn't specify that it must be done by a pastor or elder. It can be done by any other true believer. The person who has been Born Again is baptized and the substance used is water. The water symbolizes death and resurrection, and it symbolizes a new life in Christ. It also symbolizes a cleansing and a washing away of sins. Understand, the water doesn't wash away sins, it's the blood of Jesus that washes our sins away. The water is just a symbol.

When a person is water baptized, they are confessing (or should be) that they have trusted in Jesus and have been Born Again. Jesus told the apostles to make disciples and to baptize believers.

Matthew 28:19 Go ye therefore, and **teach all nations, baptizing them** in the name of the Father, and of the Son, and of the Holy Ghost:

Water Baptism is one way that you profess to the world that you are trusting in Christ and He is your Savior. You'll see that the apostles took water baptism very seriously. In the Bible, when a person professes faith in Jesus you will notice that the apostles water baptized them almost immediately. Like I've said over and over, this didn't save them, but it did show there was sincerity in their profession of faith.

Many Christians will not consider you to be a true believer if you have not been water baptized and some churches will not allow you to participate in Communion. While the baptism itself doesn't save you, there is some truth in this belief. It may be that you haven't been saved for a long time and you haven't had a good opportunity to get water baptized. On the other hand, if you claim to have been a believer for a long while and have never been water-baptized you are making an important statement. If you haven't been water-baptized, you need to ask yourself why. Is it because you don't want to publicly announce that you're a Christian? Is it because your relationship with Jesus is secondary to other things you have going on in the world or are you ashamed in some way? If you haven't been water baptized because of any of these reasons it could be a sign that you haven't truly been Born Again. When you've truly been Born Again you will not be ashamed of Jesus, and you will want people to know you belong to Him.

I said before, the apostles took water baptism very seriously. If the men who delivered to us the New Testament Scriptures, which are the basis of our Christian doctrine, thought water baptism was important then we should make it important as well. The problem we have today is that some churches don't make water baptism important enough while others try to make it a salvation issue. It's important that you understand the role water baptism plays and get water baptized for the correct reason, which is,you are water baptized to show the world that you have placed your trust in Jesus and that you have been Born Again.

Now that I've tried to show you that I am for water baptism, I want to look at just a few more verses and make sure you understand that water baptism doesn't save. Another verse in the Bible that some people misunderstand is found in Acts Chapter 2. To interpret this verse, you need to understand the context. Peter is preaching on the Day of Pentecost to Jews, many of whom had been in Jerusalem weeks earlier for Passover and had consented to the death of Jesus. After hearing Peter's sermon and realizing they were wrong about Jesus, they ask Peter "what shall we do" or in other words, what do we do now?

> Acts 2:37 Now when they heard this, they were pricked in their heart, and said unto Peter and to the rest of the apostles, Men and brethren, **what shall we do**?
>
> Acts 2:38 Then Peter said unto them, Repent, and **be baptized every one of you in the name of Jesus Christ for the remission of sins**, and ye shall receive the gift of the Holy Ghost.

When Peter says to be baptized for the remission of sins, that doesn't mean be baptized in order that your sins are removed. The word "for" never means to produce. The word "for" means in reference to or because-because of. If you buy soda for a party, the soda doesn't produce a party, but rather you are buying soda because of the party you are having. That may seem like a silly illustration but understand what Peter is saying is, be baptized because of the removal of your sins. Remember, they asked Peter what they should do, and everyone who has been Born Again should in fact be water-baptized. However, there's a big difference in what we should do and what we <u>must do</u>. It's critical for you to understand what you <u>must do</u> to be saved.

Do we have a scripture that tells us plainly what we <u>must do</u> to be saved?  In fact, we do, and it's found in Acts Chapter 16.  In this Chapter, Paul and Silas are in prison at Philippi.  While Paul and Silas are praying and singing, God sends an earthquake and opens the prison doors.  When this happened, the prison guard was about to kill himself because he knew his boss was going to kill him for letting all the prisoners escape.  However, Paul stopped him and told him not to, and no one had actually escaped or run away.  At this point, the prison guard, who would have known that Paul and Silas were in jail for being Christians, and witnessed the miracle, asks what he <u>must do</u> to be saved.  Now, understand that if God wanted you to know that you had to do anything to be saved, this is the prime place to say it.  Here we have a clear question from a gentile non-believer asking what he <u>must do </u>to be saved.

Acts 16:30 And brought them out, and said, Sirs, **what <u>must I do</u> to be saved?**

If you're a person who wants to add any form of religion to salvation, you need to understand that Paul and Silas really let you down here.  There's probably no better place in the Bible where a work such as water baptism, attending church, tithing, or any other thing you can think of to include in salvation could have been added.  However, Paul and Silas didn't add any of those things.  What did they say?

Acts 16:31 And they said, **Believe on the Lord Jesus Christ, and thou shalt be saved**, and thy house.

To be saved you must believe on Jesus, which means you place all your trust in Him and what He did to save you. If you continue to read, you'll see the man did get water baptized, but it was because he was saved and not in order to be saved. Paul was aggravated at the Corinthian Church because they were boasting about who had water baptized them and thought some were better or worse depending on who had baptized them.

> 1 Corinthians 1:12 Now this I say, that every one of you saith, I am of Paul; and I of Apollos; and I of Cephas; and I of Christ.
>
> 1 Corinthians 1:13 Is Christ divided? was Paul crucified for you? or were ye baptized in the name of Paul?

Paul was happy that he had only baptized a couple of people there.

> 1 Corinthians 1:14 **I thank God that I baptized none of you**, but Crispus and Gaius;

Paul then shows that water baptism is separate from the Gospel.

> 1 Corinthians 1:17 For Christ sent me **not to baptize, but to preach the gospel**: not with wisdom of words, lest the cross of Christ should be made of none effect.

In Chapter 4, Paul tells the Corinthians that he begot them through the gospel, or in other words they were born again after hearing his gospel message. If water baptism was involved in salvation, then Paul was making a false statement.

Paul couldn't have begotten them in the faith if water baptism was involved in their salvation, since he was not involved in their water baptism.

> 1 Corinthians 4:15 For though ye have ten thousand instructers in Christ, yet have ye not many fathers: for **in Christ Jesus I have begotten you through the gospel.**

Paul also begot Onesimus through his preaching while they were in prison together. It's hard to get water baptized while in prison. How did Paul beget Onesimus if he wasn't able to water-baptize him? Because salvation happens in the heart through faith in Jesus.

> Philemon 1:10 I beseech thee for my son Onesimus, **whom I have begotten in my bonds:**

It may seem as if I'm making too big of a deal out of whether water baptism is required for salvation. I've tried to show you that I think water baptism is very important and that it is something that every true Christian should do. The reason I'm trying to show you that it's not something you must do is because I know what the Bible says about adding any work to the Work of Christ. Remember, Paul told the Galatians that if they added circumcision to salvation, they wouldn't be saved. You must trust alone in what Jesus did for you. If the Galatians couldn't add circumcision, you can't add water baptism.

> Galatians 5:2 Behold, I Paul say unto you, that if ye be circumcised, Christ shall profit you nothing.

A Summary of the Baptisms:

| The Baptism | The Baptizer | The Recipient | The Substance | Application to you |
|---|---|---|---|---|
| The Baptism of Repentance | John the Baptist | Believers in the Messiah | Water | Not Applicable |
| The Baptism of Fire | Jesus | Non-Believers | The Lake of Fire | Not Recommended |
| Baptism Unto Moses | God | Hebrews | Moses | Not Applicable |
| The Baptism of Suffering | A Persecutor | Jesus and His followers | Suffering Pain Death | Possible but not certain or required |
| The Baptism of the Holy Ghost | Jesus | Believers in Jesus | The Holy Ghost | Not Required but Recommended |
| Believers Baptism | A Christian | Believers In Jesus | Water | Not Required but Recommended |
| **The Baptism into Christ** | **The Holy Spirit** | **Believers In Jesus** | **Jesus Christ** | **REQUIRED FOR SALVATION** |

The New Testament speaks of a doctrine of Baptisms and there are seven different baptisms described. However, it also says there is One Baptism. Why does the Bible show there are at least seven baptisms and then say there is One? The reason is, when it says One it's referring to the One that is required for you to be Saved and to be a member of the Body of Christ.

This is the Baptism into Christ that happens when you trust the Gospel with all your heart.

> Ephesians 4:4 There is **one body**, and one Spirit, even as ye are called in one hope of your calling;
>
> Ephesians 4:5 One Lord, one faith, **one baptism**,

Have you experienced the One Baptism? Have you placed your trust in Jesus and been Born Again? Has the Holy Spirit Baptized you into Christ? If so, you <u>should</u> be water-baptized to make a proclamation that you are saved and have been Born Again!

# Examine Yourself

Have you ever been around someone who says they are a Christian, but their lives don't reflect Christian beliefs or Jesus at all? First, understand that being a Christian doesn't mean that you never make mistakes or do the wrong thing. We all make mistakes, and every Christian will still sin at times and struggle against sin until we are resurrected with our new bodies. However, if we consistently live a life that is contrary to God without having an inner struggle with the Holy Spirit, then that's an indication that He's not there. You see, if you're Born Again the Holy Spirit is living inside of you. When a true Christian lives in a way that is immoral it causes the Holy Spirit inside of them grief and they feel it! Someone who thinks they're a Christian but hasn't been born again can live immorally without feeling this grief.

Ephesians 4:30 And **grieve not the holy Spirit of God**, whereby ye are sealed unto the day of redemption.

The Bible tells us to Examine Ourselves and to Prove Ourselves, that we are in the faith and that Jesus is living within us. That means we should take an internal look at ourselves and prove to ourselves that Jesus really lives in us. We just talked about feeling the grief of the Holy Spirit when we sin, which is one way we know He's there. In a previous chapter, we also saw that it's the Holy Spirit that will give you confirmation and peace, which lets you know you've truly been saved.

> 2 Corinthians 13:5 **Examine yourselves, whether ye be in the faith**; prove your own selves. Know ye not your own selves, how that Jesus Christ is in you, except ye be reprobates?

The story of Esther shows us a lot about the type of heart God is looking for and who will be His Bride. In Esther, the king represents God. In the story, the king asks his wife Vashti to come to a feast he was having with various princes and government leaders, but Vashti refuses to come. The king was proud of Vashti because she was beautiful, and he wanted to show her off basically. However, Vashti doesn't obey him and embarrasses him in front of the people at the feast. In this story, Vashti represents the Jews who disobeyed God by rejecting Jesus and the gospel. Vashti is prideful and disobedient to her husband.

When Vashti disobeys the king, he seeks a new wife. The new wife will turn out to be Esther. Esther represents the church and the Bride of Christ. Esther is also beautiful but unlike Vashti, Esther is very humble. When the king was choosing his next wife, he had them come before him, and the women were told that whatever they wanted would be given to them (think of designer clothes, bags, jewelry, etc).

> Esther 2:13 Then thus came every maiden unto the king; **whatsoever she desired was given her** to go with her out of the house of the women unto the king's house.

Unlike the other women, Esther didn't ask for any of these things.

> Esther 2:15 Now when the turn of Esther, the daughter of Abihail the uncle of Mordecai, who had taken her for his daughter, was come to go in unto the king, **she required nothing** but what Hegai the king's chamberlain, the keeper of the women, appointed. And Esther obtained favour in the sight of all them that looked upon her.

Remember, the king had been dealing with Vashti previously who was prideful, so now when he sees Esther who is beautiful but more importantly humble, he's attracted to her, and she receives his grace.

> Esther 2:17 And the king loved Esther above all the women, and **she obtained grace and favour in his sight** more than all the virgins; so that he set the royal crown upon her head, and made her queen instead of Vashti.

Like the king in this story, God seeks after humble hearts. If you're a Christian, you shouldn't be prideful and arrogant like Vashti. True Christians should be like Esther and be humble people. We shouldn't be cocky people. Peter says we should clothe ourselves with humility because it's to humble people that God gives grace.

> 1 Peter 5:5 Likewise, ye younger, submit yourselves unto the elder. Yea, all of you be subject one to another, and **be clothed with humility: for God resisteth the proud, and giveth grace to the humble**.

If you catch yourself bragging and boasting about things all the time, then you need to remember that it's humble hearts that receive grace. There's no reason for you to be boastful. We're all sinners who need God's grace and no one in their flesh is any better than others.

Another way we examine ourselves is by making sure that God is working through us and in our lives. Make no mistake, if God dwells in you, it will impact your life, and He is going to work on you and through you. God has ordained peace to His people. That means God has decided and made it sure that His people will experience peace, and one means of this peace is that they will see Him working in their lives.

Isaiah 26:12 LORD, **thou wilt ordain peace for us**: for **thou also hast wrought all our works in us.**

Not only does God ordain peace for us, but He also ordains good works to us. Not that we are doing the works, but rather He has determined He is going to do good works through us. That means God is the One doing the good works and it's not something we are trying to accomplish in our flesh in order to please Him.

Ephesians 2:10 For we are his workmanship, created in Christ Jesus **unto good works**, which **God hath before ordained that we should walk in them.**

Since God has ordained good works to His people, we can check our lives and see if He is working through us. If we have no evidence that He is working through us, then we need to ask ourselves if He is there. This is why Paul tells us to work out our salvation.

Paul doesn't say to work for your salvation but to work it out. Never try to work for salvation. To work out your salvation is to examine yourself and see if God is working through you.

Philippians 2:12 Wherefore, my beloved, as ye have always obeyed, not as in my presence only, but now much more in my absence, **work out your own salvation** with fear and trembling.

Philippians 2:13 **For it is God which worketh in you** both to will and to do of his good pleasure.

Paul realized that the work he did was the Lord working through him.

Colossians 1:29 Whereunto I also labour, **striving according to his working, which worketh in me mightily.**

If you're Born Again, God will work inside of you and there will be times that He raises up your spirit inside of you to do certain things. In the Old Testament, it was God who raised up the spirit of certain people to build the second temple. In other words, they didn't decide to do this themselves, but God was the One that caused them to do it. This is similar to how God will work in the heart of a Christian.

Ezra 1:5 Then rose up the chief of the fathers of Judah and Benjamin, and the priests, and the Levites, with all **them whose spirit God had raised,** to go up to build the house of the LORD which is in Jerusalem.

God may stir your spirit to minister to people; certain people He stirs to preach, some to teach, some to sing, and to a lot of us He just stirs our spirits to be good neighbors and live peaceful and holy lives.

If you've been Born Again, the Holy Spirit dwells inside of you and as a result of that, spiritual fruit will come out of you. This is what the Bible calls the Fruits of the Spirit. If you closely examine your heart and ask God to help you see, you should be able to tell if you have the Fruits of the Spirit.

The Fruits of the Spirit are:

Love
Joy
Peace
Longsuffering – to be patient with people without losing your cool
Gentleness
Goodness
Faith
Meekness - to be humble, mild, respectful, it's the opposite of pride
Temperance – to be moderate and have self-control

The Fruits are not the same as the Gifts of the Spirit. With the Gifts of the Spirit, God may only give one Gift to an individual. However, with the Fruits of the Spirit, God is not giving individual fruits out. The Fruits come because the Holy Spirit is inside of you, and you should have all the Fruits listed at least in some measure. It doesn't mean you'll always be loving, joyful, peaceful, but you should experience all these in some measure. If you say you have Gentleness and Goodness for example, but you never experience any peace or joy in your life, that would be a sign that you haven't been Born Again. If Jesus has saved you and you know your sins are forgiven, you should have some peace and joy in your heart regardless of your circumstances on this earth.

Every Christian will have a different amount of fruit. Don't compare yourself to others and think that because you don't have the amount of faith they do, or don't have the amount of joy they do, that you don't have the Holy Spirit. Remember that good ground and good hearts bring forth different amounts of fruit.

> Mark 4:8 And other fell on good ground, and did yield fruit that sprang up and increased; and brought forth, **some thirty, and some sixty, and some an hundred.**

If you've been Born Again and belong to Jesus, He's going to work on you your entire life to make you produce more fruit. There are people who think they belong to Him that have no fruit. Those people will be taken away, but if you belong to Him, He's going to stay with you and work on you.

> John 15:2 Every branch in me that beareth not fruit he taketh away: and **every branch that beareth fruit, he purgeth it, that it may bring forth more fruit.**

You can't produce your own fruit. If you see that you don't have fruit in your life, the answer is not to try to produce it yourself but to abide in Jesus. You abide in Jesus by trusting in Him and having a relationship with Him. If you want Heaven but you don't want a relationship with the Lord and to walk with Him, you're not Born Again.

> John 15:4 Abide in me, and I in you. As **the branch cannot bear fruit of itself, except it abide in the vine**; no more can ye, except ye abide in me.

Remember, God has ordained that those who are Born Again will have Peace and He has ordained good works to us (some more than others). To ordain means to decree or to order something. In other words, when the Bible says God ordains good works to His people, it means He's going to make sure it happens. It's not wishful thinking on God's part. When God puts His Spirit inside of you, He is going to work on you and through you. That's why James tells us that Faith Without Works is Dead.

> James 2:26 For as the body without the spirit is dead, so faith without works is dead also.

James 2:26 is a dangerous verse in the hands of a religious person who wants to involve works in salvation. It's crucial that you understand that the issue here is the Faith. It's the Faith that is dead. Adding dead works to a dead faith will produce nothing more than a dead soul. If the Holy Spirit inside of you is not the One producing the works, then all the works you try to produce in your flesh will be vain and worthless in God's eyes.

There's a difference between committing a sin and being evil. Like I've said before, Christians will struggle with sin and will sin at times as long as they are in the flesh. However, no true Christian is evil in their heart. You may have seen movies where someone is portrayed to be a Christian and then will do evil things. They'll wear a cross around their neck, murder someone in the movie, and then kiss the cross or make the sign of the cross across their chest with their fingers. The Bible tells us these people don't know God.

> 3 John:11 Beloved, follow not that which is evil, but that which is good. He that doeth good is of God: but **he that doeth evil hath not seen God.**

When we're Born Again and the Holy Ghost is inside of us, He works on our spirit in such a way that we are unable to continually walk in unrepentant sin. Jesus said that those who follow Him "shall" not walk in darkness. The word "shall" is an imperative command verb, which means the action is mandatory and not optional. The contrast to shall is "may". If I say the mail "may" come today, then I'm saying it's possible that it might come or might not come. In contrast, if I say the mail "shall" come today, I'm saying the mail is going to come and I'm not leaving room for the possibility that it might not come. This means that a true Christian will not and cannot walk in darkness.

> John 8:12 Then spake Jesus again unto them, saying, I am the light of the world: **he that followeth me shall not walk in darkness**, but shall have the light of life.

That's why if we do walk in darkness while claiming to have a relationship with Jesus, we are lying.

> 1 John 1:6 If we say that we have fellowship with him, and walk in darkness, we lie, and do not the truth:

To walk in darkness is a daily lifestyle of sin. The Bible describes your "walk" as your normal everyday way. If your daily lifestyle consists of things like committing fornication, drunkenness, covetousness, and idolatry, then you're not Born Again.

A true Christian struggles with sin. A true Christian desires to be holy and to please the Lord. A true Christian wants to walk worthy of God or in other words, we want to live a life that pleases God.

> 1 Thessalonians 2:12 That ye would walk worthy of God, who hath called you unto his kingdom and glory.

At the same time, a true Christian is aware of their sin. If a Christian claims to be perfect and sinless in their flesh, they are lying and are in the same condition as the Christian walking in darkness. Both are fooling themselves and haven't been Born Again.

> 1 John 1:8 **If we say that we have no sin, we deceive ourselves**, and the truth is not in us.

When we are Born Again, it's our spirits that are renewed. Our flesh is still dead and dying. A Christian's flesh is just as dead as anyone else's, and the greatest struggle of a Christian is against their own flesh. The Christian's flesh still lusts after things it shouldn't. It still has sexual temptations, it still wants to be prideful, still wants to be selfish, and wants to ensure its own comfort. However, the spirit of the Christian is renewed and in relationship with God. The spirit wants to be pure and wants to please God. So, what happens is, the spirit and the flesh of the true Christian are against each other. The true Christian has an internal struggle. Our flesh wants to do one thing, but our spirit says No!

> Galatians 5:17 For **the flesh lusteth against the Spirit, and the Spirit against the flesh: and these are contrary the one to the other**: so that ye cannot do the things that ye would.

Likewise, our spirit wants to do something to please God, but our flesh says No. This internal battle is something that you should be aware of if you've been a Christian for any length of time. Understand, the spirit doesn't always win these battles. Sometimes, we give in to our flesh and we sin and do things we shouldn't. However, since we have the Holy Spirit inside of us, we aren't going to continually walk in darkness.

Remember, Jesus said we'd have the light of life. When we are saved, we enter into His light. He calls us out of darkness and into the Light.

Acts 26:18 To open their eyes, and **to turn them from darkness to light**, and from the power of Satan unto God, that they may receive forgiveness of sins, and inheritance among **them which are sanctified by faith that is in me.**

Jesus is the Light and we are His children if we've truly been Born Again.

1 Thessalonians 5:5 Ye are all the children of light, and the children of the day: we are not of the night, nor of darkness.

If you've examined yourself and you aren't sure if the Holy Spirit is inside of you, you need to do a couple of things. First and foremost, make sure you understand the Gospel. Make sure you understand that salvation comes through Faith in Jesus alone and you aren't trying to add any works of the flesh to it. Secondarily, make sure that you aren't just after a ticket to Heaven. Understand, salvation is a relationship with God whereby He's active and working in your life.

I've told you before, God doesn't give you a ticket to Heaven and then leave you alone while you go live your life and live for the things of the world. God can't have a relationship with you if you're more in love with money and things than you are with Him. Remember, these things can choke God's Word so that it never affects your heart the way it should and will prevent you from being Born Again.

> Mark 4:19 And the cares of this world, and **the deceitfulness of riches**, and the lusts of other things entering in, **choke the word**, and it becometh unfruitful.

If your greatest focus in this world is on money and things, these things are your god, and your heart is with them and not with God.

> Matthew 6:21 For where your treasure is, there will your heart be also.

If your eyes are focused on Jesus, and He is your greatest treasure, you'll find His Light. If your eyes are focused on money and wealth rather than a relationship with Him, you'll stay in darkness.

> Matthew 6:22 The light of the body is the eye: if therefore thine eye be single, thy whole body shall be full of light.
>
> Matthew 6:23 But **if thine eye be evil, thy whole body shall be full of darkness.** If therefore the light that is in thee be darkness, how great is that darkness!

You must decide if you want to have a relationship with Jesus and let Him be your God, or if you want money and things to be your God. Both cannot be your primary focus or the treasure of your heart. If money is your greatest treasure, you'll do whatever it takes to have it. If God is your greatest treasure, you'll try to do what He wants primarily, and money and things of this world will always come behind Him in your list of priorities. You must choose your Master.

Matthew 6:24 **No man can serve two masters**: for either he will hate the one, and love the other; or else he will hold to the one, and despise the other. **Ye cannot serve God and mammon.**

I'm not telling you that you can't have money or even that you can't try to make a lot of money. God isn't against you having money and things. As a matter of fact, you'll see that some of God's people in the Bible such as Abraham were very wealthy. What I'm telling you is that your relationship with God must come before these things. I want you to understand that true Salvation is a relationship with God where He is your God and Master. I don't want riches and the things of this world to have a chokehold on your heart so that the Gospel is unable to sink in. I want to remove the thistles and briers that could be wrapped around your heart because I want you to be Born Again!

Is God working through you? Are the Fruits of the Spirit coming out of you? Are you walking in the Light? Does your spirit and flesh wrestle against each other? Is Jesus your Master and you want to please Him more than you want to be rich? Have you Examined yourself?

# The Lord's Passion-For You

The entire Bible is about Jesus and His redemption. It's a story about a family whose relationship was fractured and what it took to restore that relationship. When you understand this, you'll start to see God's grace, and you'll see Jesus everywhere in the Old Testament. Remember Elijah and Elisha? When Elijah met Elisha, Elisha was plowing with 12 yoke of oxen. Why 12? Because Elisha will represent Jesus in certain ways and Jesus worked with 12 Apostles.

> 1 Kings 19:19 So he departed thence, and found Elisha the son of Shaphat, who was **plowing with twelve yoke of oxen** before him, and he with the twelfth: and Elijah passed by him, and cast his mantle upon him.

John the Baptist came in the spirit of Elijah. John prepared the way for Jesus and His ministry. Likewise, Elijah came before Elisha and prepared the way for the ministry of Elisha. Elisha's ministry started at the Jordan River when he took Elijah's mantle.

The ministry of Jesus also started at the Jordan River when the Holy Spirit came upon Him.

> 2 Kings 2:13 He took up also the mantle of Elijah that fell from him, and went back, and stood by the bank of Jordan;

Below are some similarities between the miracles of Jesus and Elisha:

| Elisha | Jesus |
|--------|-------|
| Makes an iron axe head float on water | Walks on water and lets Peter walk on water |
| Turns a small amount of oil into a large amount. Also, feeds a hundred men with twenty barley loaves and a few ears of corn | Feeds 5000 men on one occasion and 4000 on another with a few loaves and fishes |
| Cures Naaman of leprosy | Cures lepers |
| Turns poison stew into good stew | Turns water into wine |
| Brings a boy back to life | Brings people back to life |

God told Abraham that he would have a child, a seed, who would bless all the nations of the earth. Abraham had a son named Isaac and Isaac had a son named Jacob. Jacob would have his name changed later to Israel. He would have 12 sons who would become the 12 tribes of Israel.

> Genesis 22:18 And **in thy seed shall all the nations of the earth be blessed**; because thou hast obeyed my voice.

Contrary to the belief of some, God was not referring to Jacob or to Israel as a nation when He said this. Rather, He was referring to one person or one descendant that would come from Abraham, and that is Jesus.

> Galatians 3:16 Now to Abraham and his seed were the promises made. He saith not, And to seeds, as of many; but as of one, **And to thy seed, which is Christ.**

In Jesus Christ, all nations of the earth have been blessed. Did you know that the Bible describes what Jesus would do and how He would bless us in the Old Testament? The Bible tells us that God would become a man and would become the Redeemer. The Redeemer is the First and He is the Last.

| Isaiah 48:12 Hearken unto me, O Jacob and Israel, my called; **I am he; I am the first, I also am the last.** | Revelation 1:8 **I am Alpha and Omega, the beginning and the ending,** saith the Lord, which is, and which was, and which is to come, the Almighty. |
| --- | --- |
| | Revelation 22:13 I am Alpha and Omega, the beginning and the end, **the first and the last**. |

The Redeemer also created the world.

| Isaiah 48:13 Mine hand also hath laid the foundation of the earth, and my right hand hath spanned the heavens: when I call unto them, they stand up together. | Colossians 1:16 For by him were all things created, that are in heaven, and that are in earth, visible and invisible, whether they be thrones, or dominions, or principalities, or powers: all things were created by him, and for him: |
|---|---|

The Redeemer is called the Holy One of Israel, who is also called the Lord thy God. The Holy One would be God and at the same time would be sent by God in the power of the Spirit.

Isaiah 48:16 Come ye near unto me, hear ye this; I have not spoken in secret from the beginning; **from the time that it was, there am I**: and now **the Lord GOD, and his Spirit, hath sent me**.

Isaiah 48:17 Thus saith the LORD, **thy Redeemer, the Holy One of Israel; I am the LORD thy God** which teacheth thee to profit, which leadeth thee by the way that thou shouldest go.

The Redeemer would be born of a woman. The woman that the Redeemer would be born of would be a virgin. The Redeemer would also be called the Son of God. The Redeemer would be God's Servant.

| Isaiah 49:1 Listen, O isles, unto me; and hearken, ye people, from far; **The LORD hath called me from the womb**; from the bowels of my mother hath he made mention of my name. | Isaiah 7:14 Therefore the Lord himself shall give you a sign; Behold, **a virgin shall conceive**, and bear a son, and shall call his name Immanuel. |
|---|---|

| Luke 1:27 **To a virgin** espoused to a man whose name was Joseph, of the house of David; and the virgin's name was Mary. | Luke 1:35 And the angel answered and said unto her, The Holy Ghost shall come upon thee, and the power of the Highest shall overshadow thee: therefore also **that holy thing which shall be born of thee shall be called the Son of God.** |
|---|---|

The Servant's mouth would be like a sharp sword.

| Isaiah 49:2 And **he hath made my mouth like a sharp sword;** in the shadow of his hand hath he hid me, and made me a polished shaft; in his quiver hath he hid me; | Revelation 19:15 And **out of his mouth goeth a sharp sword**, that with it he should smite the nations: and he shall rule them with a rod of iron: and he treadeth the winepress of the fierceness and wrath of Almighty God. |
|---|---|

Now, the Servant would be wise. He would be highly regarded, and He would be praised. Only God can receive praise but because the Servant is God, He can be praised or extolled.

| Isaiah 52:13 Behold, my servant shall deal prudently, he shall be exalted and extolled, and be very high. |
|---|

However, something was going to happen to the Servant that would be horrible. It would damage and flaw His image so badly that He wouldn't be recognizable as a man.

| Isaiah 52:14 As many were astonied at thee; **his visage was so marred** more than any man, and his form more than the sons of men: |
|---|

However, as a result of this damage, He would sprinkle the nations.

> Isaiah 52:15 **So shall he sprinkle many nations**; the kings shall shut their mouths at him: for that which had not been told them shall they see; and that which they had not heard shall they consider.

This means that He would make a blood covenant with many nations. When the first covenant was made, Moses sprinkled blood on the people as a way of confirming the covenant.

> Exodus 24:8 And Moses **took the blood, and sprinkled it on the people,** and said, Behold **the blood of the covenant**, which the LORD hath made with you concerning all these words.

Christians are sprinkled with the blood of Jesus.

> Hebrews 12:24 And to Jesus the mediator of **the new covenant**, and **to the blood of sprinkling**, that speaketh better things than that of Abel.

The Bible says the Redeemer would come to Jerusalem riding a donkey. Because of the Covenant that would be made, He would save those who joined the Covenant from Hell.

> Zechariah 9:9 Rejoice greatly, O daughter of Zion; shout, O daughter of Jerusalem: **behold, thy King cometh unto thee**: he is just, and **having salvation**; lowly, and riding upon an ass, and upon a colt the foal of an ass.
>
> Zechariah 9:11 As for thee also, **by the blood of thy covenant** I have sent forth thy prisoners **out of the pit wherein is no water**.

Someday the Saints, those who are in Covenant with the Lord, will be gathered because of His sacrifice.

Psalm 50:5 Gather my saints together unto me; **those that have made a covenant with me by sacrifice.**

It was told by Micah that Christ would be born in Bethlehem. Bethlehem was a small town about 6 miles south of Jerusalem.

Micah 5:2 But thou, **Bethlehem** Ephratah, though thou be little among the thousands of Judah, yet out of thee shall he come forth unto me that is to be ruler in Israel; whose goings forth have been from of old, from everlasting.

God chose Bethlehem as the place where He wanted Christ to be born. There are a few things that make Bethlehem special. The name Bethlehem means "House of Bread". This is significant because Jesus is the Bread of Life.

John 6:48 I am that bread of life.

Another thing that is significant about Bethlehem is that it was the place where the "Holy" Lambs were raised. The lambs that were used for sacrifice at the Temple in Jerusalem were raised in Bethlehem. The Shepherds at the Nativity scene weren't just any shepherds but were the shepherds of the holy lambs. Lastly, it was the hometown of King David, and is where Samuel anointed David to be King of Israel.

So, God became a man. He took on Himself the form of a servant. However, it wasn't just any servant or not a servant in the sense that you and I are servants. This was a special servant. He became the "Servant of the Lord" that the prophet Isaiah spoke of.

> Isaiah 42:1 **Behold my servant**, whom I uphold; mine elect, in whom my soul delighteth; **I have put my spirit upon him**: he shall bring forth judgment to the Gentiles.

The Servant would be given to the people as a Covenant!

> Isaiah 42:6 I the LORD have called thee in righteousness, and will hold thine hand, and will keep thee, **and give thee for a covenant of the people**, for a light of the Gentiles;
>
> Isaiah 49:8 Thus saith the LORD, In an acceptable time have I heard thee, and in a day of salvation have I helped thee: and I will preserve thee, **and give thee for a covenant of the people**, to establish the earth, to cause to inherit the desolate heritages;

In Isaiah, it's said that when the Messiah comes to earth miraculous things would occur. It says that blind eyes would be opened, the deaf would have their ears opened and would hear, and that lame men would walk.

> Isaiah 35:5 Then the eyes of the blind shall be opened, and the ears of the deaf shall be unstopped.
>
> Isaiah 35:6 Then shall the lame man leap as an hart, and the tongue of the dumb sing: for in the wilderness shall waters break out, and streams in the desert.

However, even with all the miracles, it was prophesied that most of the Jews wouldn't recognize the Messiah. They would see His miracles, but they wouldn't realize what was happening, and they would hear His words but wouldn't understand them.

Isaiah 6:9 And he said, Go, and tell this people, Hear ye indeed, but understand not; and see ye indeed, but perceive not.

Moreover, most of the Jews would despise and reject the Messiah.

Isaiah 53:3 **He is despised and rejected of men**; a man of sorrows, and acquainted with grief: and we hid as it were our faces from him; **he was despised, and we esteemed him not**.

The Bible says that we should Sanctify the Lord of Host. Jesus is the Lord of Host. We are to Sanctify Him in our hearts, which means we set Him apart in our hearts above everything else. In the passage below, the Jews were supposed to set apart the Lord so that He would be their fear and their dread (this applies to us also). It means we should fear Him and respect Him above anything else.

Isaiah 8:13 Sanctify the LORD of hosts himself; and let him be your fear, and let him be your dread.

It goes on to say that the Lord of Host would be a sanctuary for some, but for others, He would become a stumbling block or a rock of offense.

Isaiah 8:14 And he shall be for a sanctuary; **but for a stone of stumbling and for a rock of offence to both the houses of Israel**, for a gin and for a snare to the inhabitants of Jerusalem.

Many would stumble and fall and be broken on the stone of stumbling.

> Isaiah 8:15 And many among them shall stumble, and fall, and be broken, and be snared, and be taken.

So, the Bible says that many would be offended by the Messiah. They were offended by Him because He spoke the truth. He told them He was the only way to be saved. He told the most religious among them that they were sinners and could only be saved if they were Born Again through faith in Him. One of the reasons they didn't recognize Him as the Messiah is because they relied more on manmade traditions and what their elders had taught them than God's word.

> Isaiah 29:13 Wherefore the Lord said, Forasmuch as this people draw near me with their mouth, and with their lips do honour me, but have removed their heart far from me, **and their fear toward me is taught by the precept of men:**

So, Micah prophesied that the Judge of Israel (The Messiah) would be hit in the face with a rod.

> Micah 5:2 Now gather thyself in troops, O daughter of troops: he hath laid siege against us: **they shall smite the judge of Israel with a rod upon the cheek.**

Jesus was betrayed by His own people. The Jews turned Jesus over to the Romans, who controlled Israel at the time, to be crucified. The Romans who were trying to keep peace, gave in to the request of the Jews.

However, Pilate the Governor in charge, didn't want to crucify Jesus. Pilate's wife had a dream and she told him not to harm Jesus and that He was a Holy Man. Pilate was afraid and he thought that if he beat Jesus badly enough it would satisfy the Jews, and he wouldn't have to crucify Jesus. Isaiah had said that the Servant would be beaten, his beard would be plucked out, and He would be spat upon.

> Isaiah 50:6 I gave my back to the smiters, and my cheeks to them that plucked off the hair: I hid not my face from shame and spitting.

Even after Jesus was beaten so badly that He wasn't recognizable as a human, the Jews weren't satisfied and still demanded that Jesus was to be crucified. So, Pilate finally gave in to their request and crucified Jesus. The prophet Amos had spoken of a day when God would cause the sun to go dark at noon.

> Amos 8:9 And it shall come to pass in that day, saith the Lord GOD, that **I will cause the sun to go down at noon, and I will darken the earth in the clear day:**

At noon on the day Jesus was crucified, God darkened the sun. It was dark from noon until 3 P.M.

> Luke 23:44 And it was about the sixth hour, and **there was a darkness over all the earth until the ninth hour.**
> Luke 23:45 **And the sun was darkened,** and the veil of the temple was rent in the midst.

The crucifixion of Jesus is detailed in Psalm 22. This was written approximately 1000 years before Jesus was crucified. However, in this Psalm, God shows us how Jesus felt during the crucifixion. Remember, Jesus is both God and Man. In this Psalm, we see some of the human emotions that Jesus experienced and the pain He felt.

| Psalm 22 | |
|---|---|
| 1: **My God, my God, why hast thou forsaken me?** why art thou so far from helping me, and from the words of my roaring?<br>2: O my God, I cry in the day time, but thou hearest not; and in the night season, and am not silent. | Matthew 27:46 And about the ninth hour Jesus cried with a loud voice, saying, Eli, Eli, lama sabachthani? that is to say, **My God, my God, why hast thou forsaken me?**<br><br>(On the cross, Jesus became our sin, although He had no sin of His own. In this moment God the Father turned away from Jesus, and in His humanity, Jesus felt forsaken by His Father for the first time) |
| 3: But thou art holy, O thou that inhabitest the praises of Israel.<br>4: Our fathers trusted in thee: they trusted, and thou didst deliver them.<br>5: They cried unto thee, and were delivered: they trusted in thee, and were not confounded. | Rather than losing faith, Jesus recalls the faithfulness of God and remembers how God always delivers His people. |

| | |
|---|---|
| 6: But I am a worm, and no man; **a reproach of men, and despised of the people**. | Isaiah 53:3 **He is despised and rejected of men**; <u>a man of sorrows, and acquainted with grief:</u> and we hid as it were our faces from him; he was despised, and we esteemed him not.<br><br>(Jesus felt the rejection of His people. He felt sorrow and grief. |
| 7: All they that see me laugh me to scorn: they shoot out the lip, **they shake the head**, saying,<br>8: He trusted on the LORD that he would deliver him: **let him deliver him, seeing he delighted in him.** | Matthew 27:39 And they that passed by reviled him, **wagging their heads,**<br>Matthew 27:41 Likewise also the chief priests mocking him, with the scribes and elders, said,<br>Matthew 27:43 **He trusted in God; let him deliver him now**, if he will have him: for he said, I am the Son of God.<br><br>(He speaks of how He would be mocked when He was on the cross) |
| 9: But thou art he that took me out of the womb: thou didst make me hope when I was upon my mother's breasts.<br>10: I was cast upon thee from the womb: thou art my God from my mother's belly. | Isaiah 49:1 Listen, O isles, unto me; and hearken, ye people, from far; **The LORD hath called me from the womb**; from the bowels of my mother hath he made mention of my name<br><br>(Jesus became a Man, and as a man, He had been in relationship with the Father since He was in the womb. |

| | |
|---|---|
| 11: Be not far from me; for trouble is near; for there is none to help.<br>12: Many bulls have compassed me: strong bulls of Bashan have beset me round. | The Lord speaks of evil men who surround Him at the cross. Bashan was prime cattle country in Israel. These men were strong in the flesh. Whenever God refers to men as bulls in the Bible, He is referring to how they will be eventually killed and slaughtered, particularly during the Day of the Lord.<br><br>Isaiah 34:7 And the unicorns shall come down with them, and the bullocks with the bulls; and their land shall be soaked with blood, and their dust made fat with fatness. |
| 13: They gaped upon me with their mouths, as a ravening and a roaring lion. | The men of Judah and in particular the religious leaders, were exceptionally fierce with Jesus.<br><br>(Speaking of Jerusalem)<br>Zephaniah 3:3 **Her princes within her are roaring lions**; her judges are evening wolves; they gnaw not the bones till the morrow. |
| 14: I am poured out like water, and all my bones are out of joint: my heart is like wax; it is melted in the midst of my bowels. | Jesus speaks of how His blood has been lost, poured out. Hanging on the cross has pulled His bones out of joint. His heart and lungs are filling with fluid, and He is experiencing heart failure on the cross. |
| 15: My strength is dried up like a potsherd; and my tongue cleaveth to my jaws; and thou hast brought me into the dust of death. | Jesus has no strength left in His body at this point. He is extremely thirsty due to the loss of blood. He is on death's door |

| | |
|---|---|
| 16: For dogs have compassed me: the assembly of the wicked have inclosed me: **they pierced my hands and my feet.** | Dogs are unclean animals and refer to unclean people. In this case, these are the Roman soldiers who put the nails in the hands and the feet of Jesus. |
| 17: I may tell all my bones: they look and stare upon me. | Jesus could see His bones on His body because so much of His flesh was torn and ripped apart. |
| 18: They part my garments among them, and cast lots upon my vesture. | The Roman soldiers divided the clothes of Jesus. For His vesture which was like a coat, they cast lots, kind of like drawing straws, to see who would get it.<br><br>Matthew 27:35 And they crucified him, and parted his garments, casting lots: that it might be fulfilled which was spoken by the prophet, **They parted my garments among them, and upon my vesture did they cast lots.** |
| 19: But be not thou far from me, O LORD: O my strength, haste thee to help me.<br><br>20: Deliver my soul from the sword; my darling from the power of the dog.<br><br>21: Save me from the lion's mouth: for thou hast heard me from the horns of the unicorns. | It seemed as though the evil men who crucified the Lord had won. However, ultimately Jesus would conquer death and be delivered from the power of these men. |

| | |
|---|---|
| 22: I will declare thy name unto my brethren: **in the midst of the congregation** will I praise thee. | Because of what Jesus did on the cross, He can now dwell among His people. Those who are born again will live with the Lord forever and He will be in the midst of all His people.<br><br>Zechariah 2:11 And many nations shall be joined to the LORD in that day, **and shall be my people: and I will dwell in the midst of thee**, and thou shalt know that the LORD of hosts hath sent me unto thee. |
| 23: Ye that fear the LORD, praise him; all ye the seed of Jacob, glorify him; and fear him, all ye the seed of Israel.<br><br>24: For he hath not despised nor abhorred the affliction of the afflicted; neither hath he hid his face from him; but when he cried unto him, he heard. | We are to fear the Lord and give Him praise.<br><br><br><br><br><br>The Father heard the cry of Jesus and answered His prayers. |
| 25: My praise shall be of thee in the great congregation: I will pay my vows before them that fear him. | David who wrote this Psalm, will be in this congregation, among all the others who trust in the Messiah. |
| 26: **The meek shall eat and be satisfied:** they shall praise the LORD that seek him: **your heart shall live for ever.** | The meek, those who are humble, will eat the bread of the body of Jesus. They will be satisfied with what Jesus did on the cross for them and because of this, their souls will find eternal life. |

| | |
|---|---|
| 27: All the ends of the world shall remember and turn unto the LORD: and all the kindreds of the nations shall worship before thee. | The Gospel of Christ will go throughout the entire world and people of every nation will worship Jesus. |
| 28: For the kingdom is the LORD's: and he is the governor among the nations. | The Kingdom of Heaven is the Lord's and He will govern the world and all the nations. |
| 29: All they that be fat upon earth shall eat and worship: all they that go down to the dust shall bow before him: and none can keep alive his own soul. | All the ones that are fat on earth, that is the ones that are healthy and in good condition spiritually, will trust in and worship Jesus.<br><br>Everyone who dies will eventually bow before Him.<br>No one can keep their own soul alive. Only by trusting in Jesus can we find life. |
| 30: A seed shall serve him; **it shall be accounted to the Lord for a generation.** | When we trust in Jesus, we become children of God.<br><br>The Body of Christ is the Lord's chosen generation or chosen group of people.<br><br>1 Peter 2:9 But **ye are a chosen generation**, a royal priesthood, an holy nation, a peculiar people; that ye should shew forth the praises of him who hath called you out of darkness into his marvellous light; |
| 31: They shall come, and shall declare his righteousness unto a people that shall be born, that he hath done this. | The church will declare the righteousness of Jesus and will proclaim what Jesus did on the cross for us. |

Jesus endured terrible suffering. He shed His blood for us and died on the cross for our sins. However, God would not allow the body of Christ to see corruption, which means it wouldn't decay.

Psalm 16:10 For thou wilt not leave my soul in hell; **neither wilt thou suffer thine Holy One to see corruption.**

The prophet Hosea prophesied that on the third day, Christ would be raised from the dead.

Hosea 6:2 After two days will he revive us: **in the third day he will raise us up, and we shall live in his sight.**

The reason Hosea says he will raise us up is because Jesus died in our place. When Jesus died, we died. When Jesus rose, we rose. We are supposed to recognize that Jesus did this for us and that it was supposed to be us on the cross. So, we should realize that when Jesus rose, we rose with Him.

Ephesians 2:6 **And hath raised us up together**, and made us sit together in heavenly places in Christ Jesus:

God wants you to set aside all your pride. Simply admit that you're a sinner and that you can't live up to God's standards. If you truly want a relationship with God, trust in the Gospel with all your heart. Throw down the pride of your heart that says you can be good and please God in your flesh. Pride is dangerous and if you let it, the pride of your heart will deceive you.

> Obadiah 3 **The pride of thine heart hath deceived thee**, thou that dwellest in the clefts of the rock, whose habitation is high; that saith in his heart, Who shall bring me down to the ground?

It's far better to humble yourself now than to make Him humble you when He returns, or when you meet Him in Judgement. He's coming back and when He does, He will destroy the Kingdoms of this world and set up His Kingdom.

> Haggai 2:22 And I will overthrow the throne of kingdoms, and I will destroy the strength of the kingdoms of the heathen; and I will overthrow the chariots, and those that ride in them; and the horses and their riders shall come down, every one by the sword of his brother.

The most important thing you can do is Trust in Jesus. The Lord knows who truly Trusts in Him and those who are just playing religion. We can fool ourselves, but we will never fool the Lord.

> Nahum 1:7 The LORD is good, a strong hold in the day of trouble; and **he knoweth them that trust in him**.

The Lord is good. When we trust in Jesus we are betrothed to the Lord, and we know Him. That means we have a personal relationship with Him.

> Hosea 2:20 I will even betroth thee unto me in faithfulness: **and thou shalt know the LORD.**

The Lord is preparing a banquet for those who have put their trust in Him. His banner over them is Love which means He has shown and has proclaimed His love for them.

> Song of Solomon 2:4 He brought me to the banqueting house, and his banner over me was love.

You may feel at times that God has forgotten about you. When you feel like this, think about what Jesus did for you on the cross. Jesus still has scars on His hands where the nails were driven through them. A woman may forget about her baby, but God will never forget about you if you belong to Him.

> Isaiah 49:15 Can a woman forget her sucking child, that she should not have compassion on the son of her womb? yea, they may forget, yet will I not forget thee.
>
> Isaiah 49:16 Behold, **I have graven thee upon the palms of my hands**; thy walls are continually before me.

The Lord has born our griefs and sorrows. He was wounded because of us and our sins. We are healed because of what He did.

> Isaiah 53:4 Surely **he hath borne our griefs, and carried our sorrows**: yet we did esteem him stricken, smitten of God, and afflicted.
>
> Isaiah 53:5 But **he was wounded for our transgressions, he was bruised for our iniquities**: the chastisement of our peace was upon him; and **with his stripes we are healed**.

It pleased the Father to do this to Jesus, and Jesus did it willingly because this is the only way you could be saved.

> Isaiah 53:10 Yet **it pleased the LORD to bruise him**; he hath put him to grief: when thou shalt **make his soul an offering for sin**, he shall see his seed, he shall prolong his days, and the pleasure of the LORD shall prosper in his hand.

The sacrifice of Jesus satisfied the justice of God. What Jesus did has justified you if you're a true believer. He bore your iniquities, which means He suffered the consequences of you turning away from God.

> Isaiah 53:11 He shall see of the travail of his soul, and shall be satisfied: by his knowledge shall **my righteous servant justify many; for he shall bear their iniquities.**

Jesus did this because He loves you. He suffered and died so you could have everlasting life. Jesus is the Lamb of God. He didn't complain about going to the cross, but willingly went as our sacrifice.

> Isaiah 53:7 He was oppressed, and he was afflicted, yet he opened not his mouth: **he is brought as a lamb to the slaughter**, and as a sheep before her shearers is dumb, so he openeth not his mouth.

The Bible said He would be cut off out of the land of the living for His people's transgressions. That means He would die for our sins, for the wrongs that we committed.

> Isaiah 53:8 He was taken from prison and from judgment: and who shall declare his generation? for **he was cut off out of the land of the living: for the transgression of my people was he stricken.**

The most important thing to know in this world is to know that you've been Born Again and to know that you have a relationship with the Lord. Salvation is not about religion. It's also not just acknowledging that Jesus died and rose again as a fact. It's about what Jesus did to restore you to God and it's a restoration of a relationship. Do you want to have a relationship with the Lord? I'm not asking if you want to go to Heaven. Almost everyone wants to go to Heaven. If you truly want a relationship with the Lord, all that He requires is for you to trust in Him and His Gospel.

Admit you're a sinner who can't live up to His holy standard. Believe that Jesus is God in the flesh who came and lived the life you couldn't and that He died in your place and rose again. Add nothing else to it. Put all your trust in the Gospel of Jesus. If you truly want a relationship with God and you trust in Jesus will all your heart, He has promised to save you and give you Everlasting Life. Not because of anything you've done or will do, but because He loved you so much that He suffered and died for you.

This is the Gospel of Jesus Christ. Have you been Born Again? Have you trusted in the Gospel?

| |
|---|
| John 3:16 For God so loved the world, that he gave his only begotten Son, that whosoever believeth in him should not perish, but have everlasting life. |

Part 2
The Sure Mercies of David

The Sure Mercies of David is about the Eternal Security of the Believer. There are arguments among Christians regarding whether a person who has been Born Again is Eternally Secure or if they can lose their Salvation. The purpose of this book is to show you what the Bible says about Salvation and Eternal Security. There is nothing that will give you more peace than knowing beyond a doubt that Heaven is your home.

# Christ the Son of David

There was once a man named David who was King of Israel. David was the son of Jesse, who was from Bethlehem, and who was of the tribe of Judah. David held a special place in God's heart and God even stated that David was a man who had a heart that was like God's heart. David was a man of honour and dignity. He trusted in the Lord with all his heart. He was a loyal friend, and he was a great warrior. David was also a shepherd of sheep. He was a good shepherd who put his own life at risk to defend his sheep. A lion and a bear once tried to kill his sheep and he fought them off and killed them. God esteemed David so much that He decided that Israel's Messiah-The Christ would be born as a descendant of David.

God told David that he was going to die and go to the place where his ancestors were. However, He also told David that He was going to anoint one of David's descendants to be King, and the Kingdom of this Descendant would last forever!

> 1 Chronicles 17:11 And it shall come to pass, when thy days be expired that thou must go to be with thy fathers, that I will raise up thy seed after thee, which shall be of thy sons; and I will establish his kingdom.

God says that this Son is going to build Him a house. Many people think that God was referring to Solomon here and the temple that Solomon built. Solomon became king after David died. There's also a scripture that shows that even David thought this would be fulfilled with Solomon. However, we'll see that this scripture didn't find its ultimate fulfillment in Solomon.

> 1 Chronicles 17:12 <u>He shall build me an house,</u> and I will stablish his throne for ever.

God goes on to say that this coming King is going to be His son. This is a special title. God loved David and David held a very special place in God's heart, but even David was never referred to as God's son. He also tells David that He won't take away His mercy from Him. This is in contrast to how God took His mercy away from Saul who was king before David. Saul didn't obey God, and as a result, God took the Kingdom of Israel away from Saul and gave it to David.

> 1 Chronicles 17:13 **I will be his father, and he shall be my son**: and I will not take my mercy away from him, as I took it from him that was before thee:
>
> 1 Chronicles 17:14 But I will settle him in mine house and in my kingdom for ever: and **his throne shall be established for evermore**.

So, King David died and Solomon, who was one of David's sons, became king in his place. Solomon also held a special place in God's heart. As a matter of fact, God blessed Solomon in a very special way. God gave Solomon wisdom and made him wiser than any man on the earth. He also made Solomon richer than any man on earth. The Kingdom of Israel was in the height of its power during the reign of Solomon and Solomon built the first Temple. Before the Temple, the sacrifices and offerings had been done in a Tabernacle which resembled a large tent.

It seemed as if God's promises to David were being fulfilled in Solomon's life and in his reign. However, Solomon in all his wisdom was still just a man, and like any other man, Solomon wasn't perfect. Solomon had a ton of wives, many of whom came from other kingdoms, and many of them didn't serve the True God. Eventually, Solomon gave in to the request of some of his wives who wanted to set up altars to false gods. This angered God and God judged Solomon's Kingdom. After Solomon died, his son Rehoboam became king. During the reign of Rehoboam, God allowed a rift to happen between Rehoboam and the people which led to the Kingdom of Israel being divided. In fact, the majority of Israel followed a man named Jeroboam. Only the tribes of Judah and Benjamin remained loyal to Rehoboam. The Kingdom of Israel that seemed so glorious under Solomon was gone and instead, there were two lesser kingdoms, which were the Kingdom of Israel and the Kingdom of Judah.

Many years passed and both the Kingdoms of Israel and Judah had problems. They even went to war against each other at times which involved hundreds of thousands of casualties. Judah for the most part remained more loyal to God than Israel, and the kings of Judah all remained in David's bloodline. In contrast, the Kingdom of Israel had kings from different bloodlines and different tribes. The Kingdom of Israel worshipped other gods and was eventually taken away by the Assyrians so that only the Kingdom of Judah remained. Sadly, not too long after that, Judah was conquered by Babylon. Most of Judah's people were taken away and Solomon's Temple was destroyed. The Kingdom that started with David had come to an end. You see, God tells us that anything a man builds will come to an end. For something to last forever, it must be built by God.

> Psalm 127:1 **Except the LORD build the house, they labour in vain that build it**: except the LORD keep the city, the watchman waketh but in vain.

Although David's Kingdom was gone, his bloodline remained. The descendants of the Kings of Judah went to Babylon, but eventually through miraculous circumstances, they came back to the land of Israel. The Prophets prophesied about the Branch who would come. The Branch would be a direct descendant of King David.

> Isaiah 11:1 And there shall come forth a rod out of the stem of Jesse, and a **Branch** shall grow out of his roots:
>
> Zechariah 3:8 Hear now, O Joshua the high priest, thou, and thy fellows that sit before thee: for they are men wondered at: for, behold, **I will bring forth my servant the BRANCH.**

The Prophet Jeremiah also prophesied about the Branch. Jeremiah told us that the Branch would be King and that He would execute judgment and justice in the earth. Jeremiah also says that the name of the Branch would be "THE LORD OUR RIGHTEOUSNESS"!

Jeremiah 23:5 Behold, the days come, saith the LORD, that I will raise unto David a righteous **Branch**, and a King shall reign and prosper, and shall execute judgment and justice in the earth.

Jeremiah 23:6 In his days Judah shall be saved, and Israel shall dwell safely: and this is his name whereby he shall be called, **THE LORD OUR RIGHTEOUSNESS.**

Remember when God told David that his Descendant would build Him a house? It seemed like this was fulfilled when Solomon built the Temple but remember Solomon's Temple didn't last. Well, Zechariah prophesied that the Branch would build God's Temple!

Zechariah 6:12 And speak unto him, saying, Thus speaketh the LORD of hosts, saying, Behold the man whose name is **The BRANCH**; and he shall grow up out of his place, **and he shall build the temple of the LORD:**

If everything a man builds will eventually perish, what would make the Branch's Temple or His Kingdom last forever? If the Branch's Temple is going to last forever and if His Kingdom is going to last forever, the Branch must be God! Isaiah told us that the Son who was going to be given to Israel and who would sit on David's throne would be the Mighty God!

> Isaiah 9:6 For unto us a child is born, <u>unto us a son is given</u>: and the government shall be upon his shoulder: and **his name shall be called** Wonderful, Counsellor, **The mighty God**, The everlasting Father, The Prince of Peace.
>
> Isaiah 9:7 Of the increase of his government and peace there shall be no end, **upon the throne of David**, and upon his kingdom, to order it, and to establish it with judgment and with justice from henceforth even for ever. The zeal of the LORD of hosts will perform this.

The Branch is none other than Jesus Christ. Jesus is the Son of God who is God in human form, and He is also the Son of David who was promised to come from David. The writer of Hebrews shows us that God was referring to Jesus all along when He made His promise to David.

| Hebrews 1:5 For unto which of the angels said he at any time, Thou art my Son, this day have I begotten thee? And again, **I will be to him a Father, and he shall be to me a Son?** | 1 Chronicles 17:13 **I will be his father, and he shall be my son**: and I will not take my mercy away from him, as I took it from him that was before thee: |
|---|---|

When Jesus was on the earth there were of course people that recognized Him as the Christ. A lot of them also understood that Christ was the Son of David who was promised to come to them. There was once a blind man who begged Jesus to help him. He called Jesus the Son of David as he asked for mercy.

> Mark 10:47 And when he heard that it was Jesus of Nazareth, he began to cry out, and say, **Jesus, thou son of David**, have mercy on me.

When Jesus rode into Jerusalem there were people who cried Hosanna. Hosanna basically means "Savior please save us".

> Matthew 21:9 And the multitudes that went before, and that followed, cried, saying, **Hosanna to the son of David**: <u>Blessed is he that cometh in the name of the Lord</u>; Hosanna in the highest.

Also, notice that after they cry "Hosanna to the son of David" they say, "Blessed is he that cometh in the name of the Lord". The reason they are saying this is because they recognize that Jesus is the Lord who was sent to save them, and they are quoting from God's promises in Psalm 118.

> Psalm 118:25 **Save now, I beseech thee, O LORD**: O LORD, I beseech thee, send now prosperity.
> Psalm 118:26 **Blessed be he that cometh in the name of the LORD**: we have blessed you out of the house of the LORD.

Of course, as we've already established, this Lord who comes to save is God.

> Psalm 118:27 **God is the LORD**, which hath shewed us light: bind the sacrifice with cords, even unto the horns of the altar.

Only when the Holy Ghost gives you understanding will you fully understand that Jesus is the Lord and He is God. Jesus is not A Lord, He is THE LORD, THE LORD OF LORDS AND KING OF KINGS.

> 1 Corinthians 12:3 Wherefore I give you to understand, that no man speaking by the Spirit of God calleth Jesus accursed: and that <u>no man can say that **Jesus is the Lord**, but by the Holy Ghost.</u>

Jesus the Son of God came to earth to save us. He also came to build His Temple. Some of the Jews once asked Jesus to show them a sign. He was at the Temple (not Solomon's Temple but the rebuilt one) when they had this conversation with Him. Jesus told them the sign would be that they would destroy the Temple but that He'd raise it up in three days.

> John 2:19 Jesus answered and said unto them, Destroy this temple, and in three days I will raise it up.

The Jews didn't understand how a physical Temple could be built in three days when the one that was standing took 46 years to build.

> John 2:20 Then said the Jews, Forty and six years was this temple in building, and wilt thou rear it up in three days?

But Jesus wasn't referring to a physical Temple. He was referring to His body. You see, a Temple is a place where God's Spirit dwells. God never wanted a Temple of rocks and wood made by a man. He's always wanted to dwell inside of His people.

> John 2:21 But he spake of the temple of his body.
> John 2:22 When therefore he was risen from the dead, his disciples remembered that he had said this unto them; and they believed the scripture, and the word which Jesus had said.

Jesus is the Cornerstone of God's Temple. He is the first stone. Born Again believers make up the rest of the Temple. We are also members of the Body of Christ which is the whole of the Temple.

> Ephesians 2:20 And are built upon the foundation of the apostles and prophets, **Jesus Christ himself being the chief corner stone**;
> Ephesians 2:21 In whom all the building fitly framed together groweth unto **an holy temple in the Lord**:
> Ephesians 2:22 **In whom ye also are builded together** for an habitation of God through the Spirit.

It's hard to fathom that the God who created the universe would want His home to be inside of our bodies. However, if you've been born again that is exactly the case.

> 1 Corinthians 3:16 Know ye not that **ye are the temple of God, and that the Spirit of God dwelleth in you**?

Once you come to Christ and have been born again, you've lost ownership of your body and spirit. They now belong to God. He paid the price for you. He owns you! You're no longer the captain of the ship. The price He paid was the blood of Jesus and He fully intends to keep what He paid for!

> 1 Corinthians 6:19 What? know ye not that **your body is the temple** of the Holy Ghost which is in you, which ye have of God, and **ye are not your own?**
> 1 Corinthians 6:20 For **ye are bought with a price**: therefore glorify God in your body, and in your spirit, **which are God's**.

When you trust in Jesus and are Born Again, you become part of God's Temple. Furthermore, you enter into an Everlasting Covenant with God. What does it mean to be in an Everlasting Covenant and how long is Everlasting? Everlasting means it will never end!

| 2 Corinthians 6:16 And what agreement hath the temple of God with idols? for **ye are the temple of the living God**; as God hath said, I will dwell in them, and walk in them; and **I will be their God, and they shall be my people**. | Jeremiah 32:38 And **they shall be my people, and I will be their God:**<br><br>Jeremiah 32:40 And **I will make an everlasting covenant with them**, that I will not turn away from them, to do them good; but <u>I will put my fear in their hearts,</u> that **they shall not depart from me.** |
|---|---|

God puts His fear in the heart of His true believers which ensures they will never depart from Him. This isn't the believer hanging on to Him. This is Him hanging on to the believer! We're going to explore this more and learn more about the Everlasting Covenant. This is the Covenant of Jesus the Son of David and of Abraham!

| Matthew 1:1 The book of the generation of **Jesus Christ, the son of David**, the son of Abraham. |
|---|

# Children of the Lord

Jesus is the Son of David who was promised to come from David's lineage. Jesus had no physical children, but did you know that the Bible says that Christ would have spiritual children? We use different nouns when we refer to people depending on the context of the conversation and the nature of the relationship. For instance, you may be a father, a brother, a cousin, a son, etc depending on the context. You can be all these things at the same time, and you're not limited to one. It depends on the context of the relationship that's being referred to. It's the same way with Jesus and with our relationship to Him. In one way, we are brothers and sisters to Jesus and He is our Elder Brother. The Bible describes our relationship in that way. In another way, the Bible describes Jesus as our Husband, and believers are espoused to Christ. Jesus is God in flesh and so in another way, we are His creation. In another way, we are Children of Jesus, Children of Christ.

The Prophets said that Christ would be given children. They said that the time that He would receive His children would be when He died for their sins!

> Isaiah 53:10 Yet it pleased the LORD to bruise him; he hath put him to grief: <u>when thou shalt make his soul an offering for sin</u>, **he shall see his seed**, he shall prolong his days, and the pleasure of the LORD shall prosper in his hand.

David also prophesied of the Seed of Christ in Psalm 22. Psalm 22 talks about the crucifixion of Christ (1000 years before it happened) and at the end of Psalm 22 we learn that as a result of Christ's crucifixion, He will have a Seed that serves Him.

> Psalm 22:30 **A seed shall serve him**; <u>it shall be accounted to the Lord for a generation.</u>

God recognizes the Seed of Christ as one Generation. The Seed of Christ are Born Again Believers whom God calls a Chosen Generation and a Holy Nation!

> 1 Peter 2:9 But **ye are a chosen generation**, a royal priesthood, **an holy nation**, a peculiar people; that ye should shew forth the praises of him who hath called you out of darkness into his marvellous light;

Isaiah told us that the Children of Christ would do miracles in the land of Israel. He also said that the disciples of Christ would be given a law and testimony. The law Isaiah refers to is the New Testament Law to believe on Jesus and to love each other.

| | |
|---|---|
| Isaiah 8:16 Bind up the testimony, <u>seal the law among my disciples.</u> | 1 John 3:23 And this is his commandment, That we should <u>believe on the name of his Son Jesus Christ, and love one another,</u> as he gave us commandment.<br><br>John 13:34 A new commandment I give unto you, <u>That ye love one another</u>; as I have loved you, that ye also love one another. |
| Isaiah 8:18 Behold, **I and the children whom the LORD hath given me** <u>are for signs and for wonders in Israel</u> from the LORD of hosts, which dwelleth in mount Zion. | (The writer of Hebrews refers to these verses)<br><br>Hebrews 2:13 And again, <u>I will put my trust in him</u>. And again, **Behold I and the children which God hath given me.** |
| Isaiah 8:20 To the law and to the testimony: <u>if they speak not according to this word, it is because there is no light in them.</u><br><br>(Those who deny the Gospel have no light, in other words, no understanding and no life. When we trust in Jesus we are given understanding and life!)<br><br>(Those who have the light are Children of Light-Children of the Lord!) | John 8:12 Then spake Jesus again unto them, saying, **I am the light of the world**: he that followeth me shall not walk in darkness, <u>but shall have the light of life.</u><br><br>John 12:36 While ye have light, <u>believe in the light,</u> **that ye may be the children of light**. These things spake Jesus, and departed, and did hide himself from them. |

Isaiah shows us something special about the Seed of Christ regarding the Holy Spirit. In the Old Testament, God would send His Spirit upon men at times. It was by His Spirit that the Prophets prophesied and wrote scripture. It was also by God's Spirit that certain men such as Elijah and Elisha were able to perform miracles. The Holy Spirit was upon them, but it wasn't always permanent. He remained upon them until they accomplished the task that God wanted them to accomplish. They didn't have the indwelling of the Holy Spirit that Born Again Believers have. It's important to understand the difference between the Holy Spirit coming upon a person and the Holy Spirit dwelling within a person because in the Old Testament, you'll see the Spirit come upon men such as King Saul and then you'll see the Spirit leave that person.

God had revealed to John the Baptist that Christ would have the Spirit come upon Him, and this would be something John would see. When the Holy Spirit came upon Christ it would remain on Him. John saw the Holy Spirit come upon Jesus when Jesus came to be baptized.

---

John 1:33 And I knew him not: but he that sent me to baptize with water, the same said unto me, **Upon whom thou shalt see the Spirit descending, <u>and remaining on him</u>,** the same is he which baptizeth with the Holy Ghost.

---

Now, here's the special thing about the Seed of Christ regarding the Spirit. God made a covenant with Christ and His Seed. God says that the Spirit that is upon Christ will not leave Him. The Spirit that is upon Him will not leave nor the words in His mouth, in other words, His Testimony. But it's not just Christ, the Spirit that is upon the Seed of Christ will not leave them either! The words of their mouth will not leave either, so they won't testify that they've been saved by Jesus and then change their Testimony!

Isaiah 59:21 As for me, **this is my covenant with them**, saith the LORD; **My spirit that is upon thee, and my words which I have put in thy mouth, <u>shall not depart out of thy mouth, nor out of the mouth of thy seed, nor out of the mouth of thy seed's seed</u>**, saith the LORD, from henceforth and for ever.

If you've been Born Again, God has made a Covenant with you that the Holy Spirit will never leave you! This contrasts with what some Christians teach. However, God gives many Covenant Promises to the Believer throughout His word that proves this!

As Believers, we are not only the Seed of Christ, but we also have a Spiritual Mother. In the Bible, the citizens of a city were referred to as that city's children. Cities are always referred to as women in the Bible, never men. An example of this is in Ezekial where God is speaking to the citizens of Jerusalem and comparing them with the citizens of Sodom. Prophetically, Sodom is Jerusalem's sister, and the daughters of Sodom are the citizens of Sodom.

> Ezekiel 16:48 As I live, saith the Lord GOD, **Sodom thy sister** hath not done, **she nor her daughters**, as thou hast done, **thou and thy daughters.**

God often speaks to cities in the Bible. However, when He speaks to a city He is never speaking to the houses and streets. He is never speaking to inanimate material. Anytime God speaks to a city in the Bible He is always speaking to its citizens. Jesus once pronounced judgment on Chorazin and Bethsaida which were two cities He had visited and performed miracles in. When He spoke to these cities He was speaking to their citizens.

> Matthew 11:21 **Woe unto thee, Chorazin! woe unto thee, Bethsaida**! for if the mighty works, which were done in you, had been done in Tyre and Sidon, they would have repented long ago in sackcloth and ashes.

Likewise, He spoke to Jerusalem in the same manner referring to their unbelief. Again, He is speaking to the citizens of Jerusalem.

> Matthew 23:37 **O Jerusalem, Jerusalem**, thou that killest the prophets, and stonest them which are sent unto thee, how often would I have gathered thy children together, even as a hen gathereth her chickens under her wings, and ye would not!

The reason it's important for you to understand how God speaks to cities and their citizens is because as Believers we are also citizens of a city. However, our city is not on the earth right now. It will be one day. Our city is Heavenly Jerusalem. When a person is Born Again, they become a citizen of New Jerusalem!

Hebrews 12:22 But ye are come unto mount Sion, and unto **the city of the living God, the heavenly Jerusalem**, and to an innumerable company of angels,

It's a great thing to be a citizen of New Jerusalem but there's a little more to it than that. Do you remember that I said we have a Spiritual Mother? Our mother is New Jerusalem. It's important to understand that New Jerusalem is different than the physical Jerusalem on earth now. God speaks to Physical Jerusalem and He speaks to New Jerusalem much in the Bible. If you want to understand these verses, you must distinguish as to which one He is referring to. Physical Jerusalem that is on the earth now represents the Old Covenant while New Jerusalem represents the New Covenant in scripture.

Galatians 4:24 Which things are an allegory: **for these are the two covenants;** the one from the mount Sinai, which gendereth to bondage, which is Agar.

Galatians 4:25 For this Agar is mount Sinai in Arabia, and answereth to **Jerusalem which now is, and is in bondage with her children**.

Physical Jerusalem is in bondage to sin because most of her citizens rejected Jesus Christ. However, the citizens of New Jerusalem are free because we have trusted in Jesus and He has freed us!

> Galatians 4:26 But Jerusalem which is above is free, **which is the mother of us all.**

Christ is a Spiritual Father to the Believer and New Jerusalem is our Spiritual Mother. New Jerusalem is also the Bride of Christ. New Jerusalem represents the entire Body of Christ. Just as a man and woman become one when they are married, Jesus will become one with His Bride, the Body of Christ one day!

> Revelation 21:9 And there came unto me one of the seven angels which had the seven vials full of the seven last plagues, and talked with me, saying, Come hither, **I will shew thee the bride, the Lamb's wife.**
>
> Revelation 21:10 And he carried me away in the spirit to a great and high mountain, and shewed me **that great city, the holy Jerusalem, descending out of heaven** from God,

When that happens, New Jerusalem will take the name of Christ in the same way a woman takes a man's last name in our culture.

| Jeremiah 23:6 In his days Judah shall be saved, and Israel shall dwell safely: and this is his name whereby **he shall be called, THE LORD OUR RIGHTEOUSNESS.** | Jeremiah 33:16 In those days shall Judah be saved, and **Jerusalem** shall dwell safely: and this is the name wherewith **she** shall be called, **The LORD our righteousness.** |
|---|---|

The prophets spoke of the glory and the blessings that New Jerusalem would receive in the Old Testament. The people anxiously awaited these promises. God told them not to despair because in due time New Jerusalem would start to have children. New Jerusalem didn't have any children until after Jesus died on the cross and the New Covenant was established. Yet, God promised New Jerusalem that she would bear children one day.

> Isaiah 54:1 Sing, **O barren, thou that didst not bear**; break forth into singing, and cry aloud, thou that didst not travail with child: **for more are the children of the desolate than the children of the married wife,** saith the LORD.

Not only would New Jerusalem have children, but she would have more children than the married wife which refers to the Old Covenant and physical Jerusalem.

> Galatians 4:27 For it is written, Rejoice, thou barren that bearest not; break forth and cry, thou that travailest not: for **the desolate hath many more children than she which hath an husband.**

At the time that Isaiah wrote about New Jerusalem, she wasn't married because the New Covenant had not been established. The New Covenant was not in full force and established until after Jesus died.

> Hebrews 9:16 For where a testament is, there must also of necessity be the death of the testator.

When Jesus died, New Jerusalem started having children! God said that New Jerusalem was going to suffer the loss of the children that was supposed to have been hers, referring to most of the Jews who should have accepted Jesus but didn't. However, He said she would have other children and that there would be so many that the physical land couldn't contain them!

> Isaiah 49:20 **The children which thou shalt have, after thou hast lost the other**, shall say again in thine ears, <u>The place is too strait for me: give place to me that I may dwell.</u>

Then, New Jerusalem sees her children (prophetically speaking) and she doesn't recognize them because they don't look like Hebrews. She asks God who these people are.

> Isaiah 49:21 Then shalt **thou say in thine heart, Who hath begotten me these**, seeing I have lost my children, and am desolate, a captive, and removing to and fro? and who hath brought up these? Behold, I was left alone; **these, where had they been?**

God replies to New Jerusalem and tells her that these children that she doesn't recognize are Gentiles and that He is going to visit the Gentiles and cause them to become sons and daughters of New Jerusalem!

> Isaiah 49:22 Thus saith the Lord GOD, Behold, **I will lift up mine hand to the Gentiles**, and set up my standard to the people: and **they shall bring thy sons in their arms, and thy daughters** shall be carried upon their shoulders.

God always wanted the Gentiles to be included in His Salvation. God speaking as Christ in Isaiah, says that it will seem at first like Christ failed to gather His people. He shows that Jacob (physical Israel) will reject Him.

> Isaiah 49:5 And now, saith <u>the LORD that formed me from the womb to be his servant</u>, **to bring Jacob again to him, Though Israel be not gathered,** yet shall I be glorious in the eyes of the LORD, and my God shall be my strength.

However, He then reveals that the reason for this is because He wanted to offer salvation to the Gentiles!

> Isaiah 49:6 And he said, <u>It is a light thing that thou shouldest be my servant to raise up the tribes of Jacob, and to restore the preserved of Israel:</u> **I will also give thee for a light to the Gentiles**, that thou mayest be my salvation unto the end of the earth.

If the Jews accepted Jesus immediately, the Kingdom of Heaven would have begun and there would be no such thing as what we call the Church Age. Today we are in what many refer to as the "Church Age" which is a time frame where God is putting together the Body of Christ which is made up of Jews and Gentiles. So, God made sure that the political and religious rulers in Israel would be people who were blind to who He was. This would keep most of the Jews from also realizing who Jesus is.

> Isaiah 29:10 For the LORD hath poured out upon you the spirit of deep sleep, and **hath closed your eyes: the prophets and your rulers, the seers hath he covered.**

So, even though there are many Jews who do believe in Jesus, most of them don't yet. God is allowing this to happen so that He can have mercy on as many people as possible.

Romans 11:32 For God hath concluded them all in unbelief, that he might have mercy upon all.

When God speaks to New Jerusalem, He is speaking to her citizens. That's one of the things I established earlier. That's important because He gives many promises to New Jerusalem. God tells New Jerusalem that Christ is her Husband again in Isaiah.

| | |
|---|---|
| Isaiah 54:5 For **thy Maker is thine husband;** the LORD of hosts is his name; and thy Redeemer the Holy One of Israel; **The God of the whole earth shall he be called.** | Jesus is the Lord of Host, the Redeemer, and the Holy One of Israel. God says here that Jesus will be called the God of the whole earth! |

God goes on to tell the citizens of New Jerusalem (Born Again Christians), that He will show them Everlasting Mercy!

Isaiah 54:8 In a little wrath I hid my face from thee for a moment; but **with everlasting kindness will I have mercy on thee**, saith the LORD thy Redeemer.

God swears that He will never again be wroth with us which means extremely angry, and He will never rebuke us which means to strongly disapprove of!

Isaiah 54:9 For this is as the waters of Noah unto me: for as I have sworn that the waters of Noah should no more go over the earth; **so have I sworn that I would not be wroth with thee, nor rebuke thee.**

God also says that His kindness will NEVER depart from us. His Covenant that He establishes with us will NOT BE REMOVED!

Isaiah 54:10 For the mountains shall depart, and the hills be removed; but **my kindness shall not depart from thee, neither shall the covenant of my peace be removed**, saith the LORD that hath mercy on thee.

God tells New Jerusalem that all her children will be taught by the Lord and that they will have a great deal of peace!

Isaiah 54:13 And **all thy children shall be taught of the LORD**; and great shall be the peace of thy children.

Jesus tells us about the children who are taught by God. If you read the entire chapter (John 6) you will see that the children taught by God are those who come to Him and believe in Him. Those who profess faith but then leave were never taught by God (Jesus says this in John 6).

| John 6:45 <u>It is written in the prophets</u>, And **they shall be all taught of God**. Every man therefore that hath heard, and hath learned of the Father, cometh unto me |
|---|

| Isaiah 54:13 And **all thy children shall be taught of the** LORD; and great shall be the peace of thy children. | Jeremiah 31:34 And **they shall teach** no more every man his neighbour, and every man his brother, saying, Know the LORD: **for they shall all know me, from the least of them unto the greatest of them**, saith the LORD: for I will forgive their iniquity, and I will remember their sin no more. |
|---|---|

All the citizens of New Jerusalem have been taught by God. Also, all the citizens of New Jerusalem KNOW THE LORD. Every Born-Again person "Knows the Lord". There will be people who go to church all their lives and who do good works who were never Born Again. There will be very religious people who think they are going to Heaven who will never see it because they never totally put their trust in Jesus. They believed in Jesus in their minds, but it never sank into their heart, and they trusted that their good works contributed to their salvation. God will tell these people He never knew them because they were never Born Again. However, He will not tell anyone who has been Born Again that He never knew them because the Bible plainly tells us that ALL BORN AGAIN CHRISTIANS KNOW THE LORD!

When we put our Trust in Jesus, we become Children of the Lord. Only sinless people can be Children of the Lord; however, God gives the Seed of Christ His righteousness so that we are sinless in His eyes (not that we are sinless, but Jesus is!).

> Galatians 3:26 For ye are all the children of God by faith in Christ Jesus.

One day the Children of the Lord will go to our City and God will give us comfort there!

> Isaiah 66:13 **As one whom his mother comforteth**, so will I comfort you; and **ye shall be comforted in Jerusalem**.

# The Fountain of Living Waters

Water is essential to life. They say that our bodies are 50-75 percent water. Every part of our bodies functions better when we have plenty of water. You can't survive too long without any water. If you're ever planning a trip or activity where you're going to be outdoors or away from civilization for a good amount of time, the first thing you need to make sure you have is water. It's more important than food.

If you ever find yourself outdoors or needing water for any reason and you don't have your own water, you need to look for running water. Water that is moving is cleaner because if anything unclean falls into it, it can purify itself and push anything foul downstream. Water that isn't moving, like a puddle or pond, will collect impurities and get dirtier over time as animals use it or something unclean gets into it.

The Bible calls moving water Living Water. God often compares Himself to water in the Bible, because just as natural water sustains us and gives us life, He is the ultimate source of our life. Not only does water nourish the body but it also cleanses.

In Leviticus, God gives Israel instructions about what to do when they come into contact with unclean things. For instance, if an unclean animal such as a mouse died in your bed, your bed would be unclean. You would then have to wash it before you could use it again or else you and the bed would be unclean. If the mouse fell in a bucket of water, the water would be unclean, and you'd have to pour it out. However, if the mouse fell into a large pool of water that was fed by a spring, it would remain clean because the pool of water would be able to purify itself.

> Leviticus 11:36 Nevertheless **a fountain or pit, wherein there is plenty of water, shall be clean:** but that which toucheth their carcase shall be unclean.

Now, God is our source of life. He sustains us and He purifies us. He is the ultimate Fountain of Living Waters, for it is from Him that we have life. Our hearts beat because He makes them beat, and we breathe because He gives us air.

> Psalm 36:8 They shall be abundantly satisfied with the fatness of thy house; and **thou shalt make them drink of the river of thy pleasures**.
>
> Psalm 36:9 **For with thee is the fountain of life**: in thy light shall we see light.

In the days of Jeremiah, most of Israel had forsaken the Lord. There were different groups of people in Israel at the time of Jeremiah. There was a small group of people who still trusted in the Lord, but most of the people had forsaken Him, in other words, abandoned Him.

Jeremiah 17:13 O LORD, the hope of Israel, all that forsake thee shall be ashamed, and they that depart from me shall be written in the earth, because **they have forsaken the LORD, the fountain of living waters**.

Not only did they forsake the Lord by ceasing to Trust in Him, but they had substituted their Trust in Him for other gods and/or their own righteousness.

Jeremiah 2:13 For my people have committed two evils; **they have forsaken me the fountain of living waters,** and hewed them out cisterns, broken cisterns, that can hold no water.

God had shown Israel that He was their Fountain of Living Waters when they came out of Egypt. Remember Moses and the Rock in the wilderness? Water came out of a Rock in the desert and nourished millions of people. In Psalm 114, we learn the Rock was a flint rock.

Psalm 114:8 Which turned the rock into a standing water, **the flint into a fountain of waters.**

Paul tells us that the Rock represents Jesus!

> 1 Corinthians 10:4 And did all drink the same spiritual drink: for they drank of that spiritual Rock that followed them: **and that Rock was Christ.**

Jesus once met a woman at a well in Samaria. He asked the woman if she'd draw Him some water out of the well, which she thought was weird because He was a Jew and Jews and Samaritans didn't get along. As she is contemplating and hesitating, Jesus tells the woman that He had Living Water that He would give her and that she'd ask Him for this water if she knew who He was!

> John 4:10 Jesus answered and said unto her, If thou knewest the gift of God, and who it is that saith to thee, Give me to drink; **thou wouldest have asked of him, and he would have given thee living water.**

The woman then proceeds to ask Jesus how and where He would get this Living Water since he didn't have a bucket or anything to get water with from the well.

> John 4:11 The woman saith unto him, Sir, thou hast nothing to draw with, and the well is deep: **from whence then hast thou that living water?**

Jesus tells the woman that His water doesn't come from the well. He tells her the well water would only provide temporary sustainment.

> John 4:13 Jesus answered and said unto her, **Whosoever drinketh of this water shall thirst again:**

However, Jesus tells the woman that His water would provide Eternal Life! Whoever drinks the water that Jesus gives will NEVER thirst again! Not only that, but the water He gives will remain in that person and will become a well that is spring fed, and it will last ETERNALLY!

> John 4:14 But **whosoever drinketh of the water that I shall give him shall <u>never</u> thirst**; but the water that I shall give him shall be in him **a well of water springing up into everlasting life**.

When you Trust in Jesus and are Born Again, God has promised you will never hunger or thirst again. If you were Born Again but were somehow able to lose your salvation these verses wouldn't be true. If you truly drank of the water Jesus gives, but then later thirsted, God's word wouldn't be accurate.

| John 6:35 And Jesus said unto them, I am the bread of life: he that cometh to me **shall <u>never</u> hunger**; and he that believeth on me **shall <u>never</u> thirst**. | Isaiah 49:10 **They shall not hunger nor thirst**; neither shall the heat nor sun smite them: for he that hath mercy on them shall lead them, **even by the springs of water shall he guide them.** |
|---|---|

The opponent of this doctrine would tell you that you must keep drinking. In other words, it's not just one drink, but you keep yourself in good graces with God by your good works. However, that's the opposite of what Jesus teaches. We don't keep drinking by our good works, we keep drinking because of the Fountain of Living Water that Jesus puts in our spirit!

You see, Jesus tells us that this Water is the Holy Spirit that will be inside of the Believer! In Isaiah, we are shown that these waters will not fail, in other words, the water doesn't stop flowing!

Isaiah 58:11 And the LORD shall guide thee continually, and satisfy thy soul in drought, and make fat thy bones: **and thou shalt be like a watered garden, and like a spring of water, whose waters fail not.**

Jesus offers His water to anyone who is thirsty.

John 7:37 In the last day, that great day of the feast, Jesus stood and cried, saying, **If any man thirst, let him come unto me, and drink**.

Jesus then refers to Isaiah and the water that will flow out of the person who puts their Trust in Him.

John 7:38 **He that believeth on me**, as the scripture hath said, **out of his belly shall flow rivers of living water.**

The Apostle John who penned this quote, then tells us that Jesus was referring to the Holy Spirit. This means the Holy Spirit inside of the Believer is the Eternal Spring of Water. However, this was not available until after Jesus rose from the dead. This is only available to Born Again Believers.

John 7:39 (**But this spake he of the Spirit**, which they that believe **on him should receive**: for the Holy Ghost was not yet given; because that Jesus was not yet glorified.)

Now, we remember that in addition to water giving us life and drink, it also cleanses us. We as sinners, require cleansing and the Lord must wash us. The Lord promises His people that He will cleanse them from their sins if they Trust in Him.

Isaiah 1:18 Come now, and let us reason together, saith the LORD: **though your sins be as scarlet, they shall be as white as snow**; though they be red like crimson, they shall be as wool.

The Lord promises He will wash our sins away so that our souls are as white as snow.

Psalm 51:2 **Wash me** throughly from mine iniquity, and cleanse me from my sin.
Psalm 51:7 Purge me with hyssop, and I shall be clean: **wash me, and I shall be whiter than snow.**

Only the Lord can wash us. Job knew that he couldn't make himself clean in God's eyes. You can't get clean through religion. It won't work. You'll never be clean enough. Anyone who tries to come to God by cleaning up their life in the power of their flesh will be plunged into a ditch (thrown into hell).

Job 9:30 **If I wash myself with snow water**, and make my hands never so clean;

Job 9:31 **Yet shalt thou plunge me in the ditch**, and mine own clothes shall abhor me.

To be in God's presence we must be washed with pure water. Jesus is the only One who can wash our sins away. The prophets told of this cleansing that God would provide, and the New Testament shows us that it would come through faith in Jesus.

| Hebrews 10:22 Let us draw near with a true heart in full assurance of faith, having our hearts sprinkled from an evil conscience, **and our bodies washed with pure water.** | Ezekiel 36:25 **Then will I sprinkle clean water upon you, and ye shall be clean**: from all your filthiness, and from all your idols, will I cleanse you. |
|---|---|

Not long before Jesus went to the cross, He washed His disciples' feet. When He did this, He established a few important principles. First, to be in a relationship with Him, He must wash you (cleanse you from your sins).

John 13:8 Peter saith unto him, Thou shalt never wash my feet. Jesus answered him, **If I wash thee not, thou hast no part with me.**

Second, when Jesus washes you, you are completely clean. You do not need to wash yourself at this point because He says He has totally and completely cleansed you!

John 13:10 Jesus saith to him, **He that is washed** needeth not save **to** wash his feet, **but is clean every whit:** and ye are clean, but not all.

Lastly, Jesus establishes the principle of feet washing. When we walk in the world our feet get dirty both literally and figuratively. Jesus told His disciples to wash each other's feet. This isn't just about keeping our feet clean literally, but more so about keeping each other accountable and clean from the moral pollutions of the world.

> John 13:10 Jesus saith to him, He that is washed **needeth not save to wash his feet,** but is clean every whit: and ye are clean, but not all.
>
> John 13:14 If I then, your Lord and Master, have washed your feet; **ye also ought to wash one another's feet.**

Remember, this has nothing to do with keeping us saved. Jesus already provided the complete cleansing. He completely cleansed our spirit. We hold each other accountable as Christians for the sake of the Church and to help each other walk through this sinful world.

Jesus is the Fountain of Living Waters. He is the source, the Fountain from which the Living Water flows. The Living Water that comes from Him is the Holy Spirit which becomes an Eternal Spring or Eternal source of Life within the Believer. Remember, we learned in Leviticus that if a mouse were to fall in a well of water that was fed by a spring, it would remain clean? The spring or fountain would cleanse the body of water and flush out the impurities. That's what the Holy Spirit does inside of the Believer. The Holy Spirit inside of the Believer is like a spring of water. The Bible says the Holy Spirit renews the Believer. To renew something is to restore it and to make it like new.

| Titus 3:5 Not by works of righteousness which we have done, but according to his mercy he saved us, **by the <u>washing</u> of regeneration, and <u>renewing</u> of the Holy Ghost;** | The washing of regeneration is our spirit being regenerated or brought back to life by the Holy Spirit.<br><br>The renewing of the Holy Ghost is what the Holy Spirit/Ghost does inside of the Believer. Remember, He's the Spring of Water that flushes out the impurities and keeps us alive with a never-ending supply of water. |
|---|---|

Our physical bodies are in a state of decay. They are literally dying and wasting away. However, the Holy Spirit inside of the Believer renews the Spirit of the Believer every day! He is constantly restoring us spiritually! He flushes out the bad things that come in and gives us Living Water!

2 Corinthians 4:16 For which cause we faint not; but though our outward man perish, yet **the inward man is renewed day by day**.

One drink from the Fountain of Living Waters provides Eternal Life. A person drinks from the Fountain of Living Waters when they Trust in the Blood of Jesus and are Born Again. Eternal Life is Eternal… If we were saved but could lose our salvation, we could never have possessed "Eternal" life. At best, we could have been given life if that were the case. If you possess Eternal Life, it must continue Eternally or it was never Eternal Life.

Jesus said that those who believe in Him would NEVER die. Even though they died physically they would still be alive. That means our loved ones who have passed away but have Trusted in Jesus and were Born Again are still alive!

John 11:25 Jesus said unto her, I am the resurrection, and the life: **he that believeth in me, though he were dead, yet shall he live**:

Furthermore, those who have been Born Again and are still physically alive SHALL NEVER DIE!

John 11:26 And **whosoever liveth and believeth in me <u>shall never die</u>**. Believest thou this?

If someone was truly Born Again through Faith in Jesus but then lost their Salvation, then the statement Jesus made in John 11:26 would not be totally accurate. In that case, the person would have believed in Jesus but died in contrast to the statement that Jesus made. However, I will tell you that the statement is totally accurate and that Salvation is Forever and Eternal!

# David's Mercies

Has anyone ever shown you Mercy?  To be shown Mercy is to be spared some treatment or punishment that you had coming to you so to speak, or to be shown compassion or leniency when it was otherwise within someone's power to punish you.  Mercy is not for innocent people but for the guilty.  An example of Mercy is when a police officer is about to give you a speeding ticket but then decides to show you a little compassion and lets you off with a warning.

We talked about Living Water in the previous chapter.  The Bible says this Water is available to anyone who is thirsty for it.  The Bible also tells us that the Water is free.  You don't need any money for the Water!

Isaiah 55:1 Ho, **every one that thirsteth, come ye to the waters, and he that hath no money**; come ye, buy, and eat; yea, come, buy wine and milk without money and without price.

God also tells us to listen to what He has to say. If we hear His message, it will cause our Souls to live! Furthermore, He says that He will make an Everlasting Covenant with us. This Covenant is not to a Nation, but rather it is to whomever is thirsty for it. The nature of the Covenant He offers to the individual is that it is Everlasting, which means it will last Eternally. Furthermore, the person with whom He makes the Covenant with shall receive the <u>Sure Mercies of David</u>.

---

Isaiah 55:3 Incline your ear, and come unto me: <u>hear, and your soul shall live</u>; and **I will make an everlasting covenant with you, even the sure mercies of David.**

---

This Covenant is the New Covenant the Prophets spoke of, and Paul tells us this Covenant came into power when Jesus rose from the dead, which is also what we are told in other New Testament books regarding the New Covenant.

---

Acts 13:34 And as concerning that he raised him up from the dead, now no more to return to corruption, **he said on this wise, I will give you the sure mercies of David.**

---

All Born Again Christians receive the Sure Mercies of David. If God has given us the Sure Mercies of David, we need to find out what this entails. First, let's define the word "Sure". We often use the term "sure thing" in our society but often when we say sure thing, it's not sure at all. The word "Sure" means to be certain, positively confident, to have no doubt, or to be inevitable. In other words, the Born Again Believer is positively certain to receive the Mercies of David.

David's Mercies are described in the Old Testament. Now, David was a top-notch guy. Please understand, as a man David was right up there with the best morally speaking. However, David wasn't perfect. The only Perfect Man that has walked the earth is Jesus. Even men who love the Lord and have a relationship with Him, are flawed in the flesh. Even men who love the Lord can sin grotesquely at times. They won't walk in those sins and live a lifestyle of disobedience to God, but they can and do have moral failures.

David had a moral failure at a point in his life and sinned against God. As a matter of fact, the sins that David committed during that period are the kind of sins that bring severe judgment and chastisement from God. God had previously taken the lives of men in the Old Testament for committing lesser sins than those that David committed during this time. David understood this and he cried out to God, begging for His Mercy.

Psalm 51:1 **Have mercy upon me, O God**, according to thy lovingkindness: according unto the multitude of thy tender mercies **blot out my transgressions**.

Psalm 51:11 Cast me not away from thy presence; and take not thy holy spirit from me.

God spoke to David through the Prophet Nathan and told David that his sin had been put away and that he would not die. However, God did punish David for his sins and David suffered greatly. Nonetheless, God forgave David and remained in relationship with him.

> 2 Samuel 12:13 And David said unto Nathan, I have sinned against the LORD. And Nathan said unto David, **The LORD also hath put away thy sin; thou shalt not die.**

When God told David that He put away his sin, David understood that God was providing an atonement for him. David also understood that while he was guilty, God was not imputing his sins to his account. The atonement that God provided for David was the blood of Jesus, and He applied Jesus's blood to David as payment for David's sins. David's response to God's Mercy was gratitude and a realization that he was Blessed.

> Psalm 32:1 **Blessed** is he whose transgression is forgiven, **whose sin is covered**.
> Psalm 32:2 **Blessed** is the man unto whom the LORD **imputeth not iniquity**, and in whose spirit there is no guile.

The Apostle Paul tells us that the Born-Again Believer is Blessed in the same manner as David.

> Romans 4:6 Even as David also describeth **the blessedness of the man, unto whom God imputeth righteousness without works,**
> Romans 4:7 Saying, Blessed are they whose iniquities are forgiven, and whose sins are covered.
> Romans 4:8 **Blessed is the man to whom the Lord <u>will not</u> impute sin**.

You see, he doesn't say Blessed is the man who does not sin. As long as we're in the flesh, we all have some magnitude of sin. The issue for the Believer is that the Lord is not imputing sin to the Believer's account.

It was a great blessing to David when God showed him Mercy, after his moral failure. However, this wasn't the only Mercy that God showed to David. In fact, there were other mercies given to David that were even more of a blessing to him, and David sings about these mercies in Psalm 89.

> Psalm 89:1 **I will sing of the mercies of the LORD** for ever: with my mouth will I make known thy faithfulness to all generations.
>
> Psalm 89:2 For I have said, **Mercy shall be built up for ever**: thy faithfulness shalt thou establish in the very heavens.

The reason these mercies are so important to David is because they extend to his seed which is his Son. God made a covenant with David regarding a Son that he was going to have with whom God would give an Everlasting Kingdom to.

> Psalm 89:3 **I have made a covenant with my chosen**, I have sworn unto David my servant,
> Psalm 89:4 Thy seed will I establish for ever, and build up thy throne to all generations. Selah.

At this point, we need to understand something about how the Bible refers to the Messiah, which we know is Jesus. In the Old Testament, the Messiah is sometimes called David because he is the Son of David. When the Old Testament prophets referred to the Son of David or the "Greater David", He would simply be called David. Understand, these were written hundreds of years after David the son of Jesse had already died.

| | | |
|---|---|---|
| Jeremiah 30:9 But they shall serve the LORD their God, and **David their king, whom I will raise up unto them**. | Hosea 3:5 Afterward shall the children of Israel return, and seek the LORD their God, **and David their king**; and shall fear the LORD and his goodness in the latter days. | Ezekiel 37:24 **And David my servant shall be king over them;** and they all shall have one shepherd: they shall also walk in my judgments, and observe my statutes, and do them. |

It's important to understand how the scriptures speak of the Messiah and call him David because, in Psalm 89, David writes about the Son of David and calls him David, although he is not referring to himself but the Messiah. David had a vision about God anointing the Messiah.

Psalm 89:19 Then thou spakest in vision to thy holy one, and saidst, I have laid help upon one that is mighty; **I have exalted one chosen out of the people.**
Psalm 89:20 I have found David my servant; with my holy oil have I anointed him:

We know God is speaking of Christ here because of the way He is described. Among other things, God says that He (Christ) will be God's Firstborn who is higher than the kings of the earth.

Psalm 89:27 Also **I will make him my firstborn**, higher than the kings of the earth.

God then references the Covenant, which was originally spoken to David, however we see that God's Mercy is going to extend to the Seed of Christ!

> Psalm 89:28 **My mercy will I keep for him for evermore**, and my covenant shall stand fast with him.
>
> Psalm 89:29 **His seed also will I make to endure for ever**, and his throne as the days of heaven.

Why would Christ need Mercy? Christ doesn't need Mercy for Himself because He is the Sinless and the Perfect Son of God. However, the Seed of Christ does need Mercy and we will see how God's Mercy extends to Christ's Seed!

> Psalm 89:30 **If his children forsake my law**, and walk not in my judgments;
>
> Psalm 89:31 If they break my statutes, and **keep not my commandments;**
>
> Psalm 89:32 **Then will I visit their transgression with the rod**, and their iniquity with stripes.
>
> Psalm 89:33 **Nevertheless my lovingkindness will I not utterly take from him, nor suffer my faithfulness to fail.**

God says that when the Seed of Christ sins, He will chastise them. However, He will not send them to Hell! God goes on to make a promise and establish the security of Christ's Seed.

Psalm 89:34 **My covenant will I not break**, nor alter the thing that is gone out of my lips.

Psalm 89:35 **Once have I sworn by my holiness** that I will not lie unto David.

Psalm 89:36 **His seed shall endure for ever**, and his throne as the sun before me.

Psalm 89:37 It shall be established for ever as the moon, and as a faithful witness in heaven. Selah.

GOD HAS MADE A COVENANT PROMISE THAT THE SEED OF CHRIST WILL ENDURE! HE HAS SWORN BY HIS HOLINESS! This section ends with verse 37 and the last word is "Selah" which means "think or meditate on this".

As flesh and blood people, it's hard for us to grasp the Mercy of God. You see, our Mercy is limited. The way most of us think is that we can take so much but eventually Mercy will run out. Some Christians think that God will show Mercy for a while but eventually, He is going to get fed up and His Mercy will expire. However, David understood that God's Mercy Endures Forever.

Psalm 100:5 For the LORD is good; **his mercy is everlasting**; and his truth endureth to all generations.

Psalm 118:1 O give thanks unto the LORD; for he is good: **because his mercy endureth for ever.**

Abraham is known as the Father of Faith and the model of those who would put their Trust in the Lord and who would be counted Righteous because of their Faith and Trust rather than their works. Those of us who Trust in Jesus are spiritual children of Abraham.

Galatians 3:7 Know ye therefore that **they which are of faith, the same are the children of Abraham.**

David is a model of the New Testament Believer and of the Mercy that God extends to the Believer. Jesus Christ came in the flesh as the Son of David.

Romans 1:3 Concerning his Son Jesus Christ our Lord, **which was made of the seed of David according to the flesh;**

When Jesus conquered life and death, He secured Everlasting Mercy for His children.

Hebrews 2:13 And again, I will put my trust in him. And again, **Behold I and the children which God hath given me.**
Hebrews 2:14 **Forasmuch then as the children are partakers of flesh and blood, he also himself likewise took part of the same;** that through death he might destroy him that had the power of death, that is, the devil;
Hebrews 2:17 Wherefore in all things it behoved him to be made like unto his brethren, **that he might be a <u>merciful</u> and faithful high priest** in things pertaining to God, **to make reconciliation for the sins of the people.**

As the Seed of Christ, the Born-Again Believer is promised EVERLASTING MERCY!

# Chastised Children

God has given His Children Everlasting Mercy.    If we truly understood how much Mercy we have been given we would all live more holy than we do.  Paul begs the Romans to live holy lives because of the Mercy that they've been shown, and he also tells them it's only reasonable that they do this service.  In other words, due to the Mercy that they've been given, it only makes good sense for them to present their lives as a living sacrifice to God by living holy.

Romans 12:1 I beseech you therefore, brethren, **by the mercies of God**, that ye present your bodies a living sacrifice, holy, acceptable unto God, **which is your reasonable service**.

The problem that we have as Christians is that although our spirits are reborn, we are still in a body of flesh that is prone to sin.  Our flesh isn't reborn and so our spirit and our flesh are at odds with each other.  Because of this, we can't be perfect as long as we're in these bodies.  Along with the voice of the Spirit, God the Father has promised to chastise His children when they sin.

Remember God's promise to David and to the Seed of Christ. When we sin, God has promised that our transgression is going to be visited with the rod.

> Psalm 89:31 If they break my statutes, and keep not my commandments;
> Psalm 89:32 **Then will I visit their transgression with the rod**, and their iniquity with stripes.

When God speaks of using the rod you may think that sounds harsh, especially today, but it's an act of love. In fact, God says that those who spare the rod for their children hate them. One of the reasons that society is in such a mess today is that children grow up without a healthy reverence and respect for anything. When children learn that there are going to be negative consequences for immoral behavior, they become better people and better citizens. The Bible doesn't advocate abuse or physically harming a child. What we're talking about is sensible discipline.

> Proverbs 13:24 He that spareth his rod hateth his son: but **he that loveth him chasteneth him betimes.**

God makes a division in His word between how He judges the world and how He judges His children. You see, normally parents only chastise their own kids. If you go around spanking other people's kids, then you're bound to run into trouble and eventually receive a spanking of your own. God only chastises His children, those who have been Born-Again and are Children of the Lord.

The rest of the world will be judged and punished accordingly someday. However, for now, God doesn't provide spiritual correction in their lives. If God never provides spiritual correction, then you're not His child.

> Hebrews 12:7 **If ye endure chastening, God dealeth with you as with sons**; for what son is he whom the father chasteneth not?
>
> Hebrews 12:8 **But if ye be without chastisement**, whereof all are partakers, **then are ye bastards, and not sons**.

It's never fun to receive a spanking or to receive correction from someone. However, sometimes you can look back and see how that correction was beneficial in your life. If God is chastising you, then you are Blessed! That means He cares about you, and He cares about what is going on in your life.

> Psalm 94:12 **Blessed is the man whom thou chastenest**, O LORD, and teachest him out of thy law;

When you understand that God is taking action and correcting you, it should make you happy. Although it's painful in the moment, this is proof your Father in Heaven loves you and sees you!

> Job 5:17 Behold, **happy is the man whom God correcteth**: therefore despise not thou the chastening of the Almighty:

We shouldn't get angry when the Lord disciplines us or grow weary as if it's some dreadful thing that is happening. God is teaching us to be more like Him.

Proverbs 3:11 My son, despise not the chastening of the LORD; neither be weary of his correction:

Proverbs 3:12 **For whom the LORD loveth he correcteth**; even as a father the son in whom he delighteth.

God chastises His children for their profit and so they might be more like Him. It's in our best interest to live like God wants. Sin brings nothing but pain. We may think it's fun at the time, however, sin will always cause destruction in your life. It will never make anything better for you. God doesn't chastise His kids because He wants to hurt them but to help them.

Hebrews 12:10 For they verily for a few days chastened us after their own pleasure; **but he for our profit, that we might be partakers of his holiness.**

Hebrews 12:11 Now no chastening for the present seemeth to be joyous, but grievous: nevertheless **afterward it yieldeth the peaceable fruit of righteousness unto them which are exercised thereby.**

We could avoid some pain and prevent some spiritual correction if we'd use a little more common sense at times and make proper judgments in our lives.

We need to learn from our mistakes. We also need to read our Bibles more so that we know more about what God desires for us. God says if we'd use better judgment at times, we could prevent Him from having to chastise us.

1 Corinthians 11:31 For if we would judge ourselves, we should not be judged.

However, on the same note, God wants us to know that when He does judge us for doing something wrong, He chastens us as children and doesn't judge us in the same manner that He judges the world.

1 Corinthians 11:32 But **when we are judged, we are chastened of the Lord**, that we should not be condemned with the world.

It's important for you to know that you can spare yourself some pain because at times God's chastisement can be very painful even though it is ultimately for our good. As a Christian, you will be tempted to walk after the lust of your flesh. All people reap what they sow in one manner or another. Just because God doesn't deal with a Born-Again person the same way He deals with other people doesn't mean there are no consequences.

Galatians 6:7 Be not deceived; God is not mocked: for whatsoever a man soweth, that shall he also reap.

If you sow to your flesh as a Christian, you're going to have problems with your flesh, with your physical body. This is one of God's promises to His people. Sowing to your flesh means you're giving the flesh what it wants. We're not talking about taking care of your body. God wants us to do that. We're talking about giving in to the sinful desires of the flesh such as committing fornication, which is just one example. God says that when we do this, we're going to reap corruption in our flesh. This means we're going to have physical issues such as sickness and even death. However, to the Born-Again Christian, the judgment is confined to our flesh. Our spirits remain saved and Born-Again.

Galatians 6:8 For **he that soweth to his flesh <u>shall of the flesh</u> reap corruption**; but he that soweth to the Spirit shall of the Spirit reap life everlasting.

God pronounced judgment on our sins at the cross. The Believer's flesh is still under condemnation, but our spirits and souls are free when we are in Jesus.

Romans 8:3 For what the law could not do, in that it was weak through the flesh, **God sending his own Son** in the likeness of sinful flesh, and for sin, **condemned sin in the flesh**:

God's chastisement can be so severe at times, that the recipient dies physically. This type of severe chastisement is usually reserved for people who cause damage to the Body of Christ and mar the name of the Church.

God doesn't take any pleasure in cutting a Believer's life short, but we have to understand that could be necessary and worthwhile in the long run if we damage the Church's image. The world needs to see a Holy Church in order to realize we're different and to see Jesus in us.

In Corinth, some of the members of the Church were getting drunk when taking Communion. Some of them were being gluttonous and not thinking about others during this time. They didn't have their thoughts focused on Jesus but were just enjoying the meal and thinking about themselves and their pleasure. As a result of this, God chastised them and some of them died physically. Understand, they were true Believers, and that's why God chastised them. Also understand, they didn't lose their Salvation! Paul says they slept, which is a New Testament term used several times to describe a Christian who has died physically and refers to their physical body. It never refers to a lost person.

1 Corinthians 11:30 **For this cause** many are weak and sickly among you, **and many sleep**.

Another example of severe chastisement is found in Corinthians. There was a man in the Church who was having a sexual relationship with his stepmother. Paul told the Church they needed to deliver him to Satan, which is a fancy way of saying they needed to kick him out of the Church and back into the world "Satan's Kingdom". You see, the man was marring the name and image of the Church, which could prevent others from becoming Christians. Also, the things he was doing were evidence that he might not have been truly Born-Again.

So, Paul says to kick him out of the church for the destruction of his flesh. If he was truly saved and continued in his sin, Paul was confident that the man's flesh would be destroyed. If he wasn't truly saved, this action may be what it took to give the man a reality check and make him examine his heart and "work out his salvation", which in turn could result in his salvation. That's why Paul says, "so that his spirit may be saved".

> 1 Corinthians 5:5 To deliver such an one unto Satan **for the destruction of the flesh, that the spirit may be saved** in the day of the Lord Jesus.

Most churches don't exorcise this type of discipline today which is why there's a lot of ungodliness in many churches. The Apostle Paul taught his churches to exercise church discipline and to not have fellowship with someone who claimed to be a Christian but was living immorally.

You may have heard the term "license to sin" used by someone who rejects Eternal Security. The idea is that if we are Eternally secure once we've been Born Again, we'd have a "license" to sin all we want as if there would be no consequence to our sin. This is a statement of ignorance to God's Word. Anyone who has read their Bible should know why this is an ignorant statement because the Bible is full of examples showing us the consequences people who were in a relationship with God faced when they sinned. Even though these people didn't lose their Salvation "because they were saved by grace through faith", they suffered greatly because of their sin.

When Israel left Egypt and approached the Promised Land, they feared entering the land and didn't trust the Lord the way they should have. This angered the Lord and He expressed His anger to Moses. Moses begged God to forgive the people and the Lord did.

> Numbers 14:19 **Pardon, I beseech thee**, the iniquity of this people **according unto the greatness of thy mercy**, and as thou hast forgiven this people, from Egypt even until now.
> Numbers 14:20 **And the LORD said, I have pardoned** according to thy word:

However, even though God forgave their sin, that didn't mean there weren't any consequences for their actions. God pardoned their sin. Nevertheless, He also chastised them, and as a consequence for their sin, all the people over 20 years old (with exception of Joshua and Caleb) died in the wilderness and never entered the Promised Land. Their children and the younger people were the ones who entered the land.

> Numbers 14:29 **Your carcases shall fall in this wilderness**; and all that were numbered of you, according to your whole number, from twenty years old and upward which have murmured against me.

When David sinned, God forgave David. However, like Israel, David suffered greatly because of his sin. Remember, when we damage the image of the church God is likely to chasten us severely. David damaged the image of Israel with his sin and one judgment was that David's child died.

> 2 Samuel 12:14 Howbeit, because **by this deed thou hast given great occasion to the enemies of the LORD to blaspheme**, the child also that is born unto thee shall surely die.

This wasn't the only judgment and chastening that David received. As a result of David's sin, he had family trouble for the rest of his life. David's sin caused a chain reaction and two more of David's sons died. One of David's sons murdered his other son and then that son was killed because of vengeance. David's sons were responsible for their actions. However, had David not sinned he would have held a higher reputation with them, and they may have confided in him and not have done what they did. David wept severely when his first son died.

> 2 Samuel 13:36 And it came to pass, as soon as he had made an end of speaking, that, behold, the king's sons came, and lifted up their voice and wept: and **the king also and all his servants wept very sore.**

When Absalom the second son died, David was completely broken.

> 2 Samuel 18:33 And the king was much moved, and went up to the chamber over the gate, and wept: and as he went, thus he said, **O my son Absalom, my son, my son Absalom! would God I had died for thee, O Absalom, my son, my son!**

After David sinned, God told him the sword would never depart his house, which referred to the family problems he was going to suffer.

> 2 Samuel 12:10 **Now therefore the sword shall never depart from thine house**; because thou hast despised me, and hast taken the wife of Uriah the Hittite to be thy wife.

Do you think that David felt like he got away with his sin? Do you think that since God showed David mercy and forgave him, David felt like there weren't any consequences? Do you think David felt like he had a license to sin? Our sin doesn't just affect ourselves. It hurts other people, and it may be the difference in whether someone gets saved. If you damage your reputation with a person, you could lose your influence and no longer be able to be a witness in that person's life. This could be the difference in whether or not someone turns to Jesus.

Sometimes God must chasten His people severely. He does this because He loves us. He also does this because He wants other people to be saved through our influence. Ultimately, God is trying to save as many people as possible and when our actions get in the way of that, we will have problems. Nevertheless, though we are chastened severely, God will not deliver us over to death. We will not go to Hell if we've truly been Born Again.

| Psalm 118:18 The LORD hath chastened me sore: **but he hath not given me over unto death.** |
| --- |

# 5 Crowns

To understand what the Bible says about Salvation, it's crucial you understand the difference between a Gift and a Reward. A Gift by definition, is something that someone freely or voluntarily gives you, which is not compensation. A Reward, on the other hand, is something that is given in return for something, in other words, it is compensation. The Bible clearly tells us that Salvation is a <u>Free Gift</u> from God. That means Salvation is in no way a means of God compensating us for our good actions.

| Romans 5:16 And not as it was by one that sinned, so is the gift: for the judgment was by one to condemnation, but **the free gift** is of many offences unto justification. | Romans 6:23 For the wages of sin is death; but **the gift of God is eternal life** through Jesus Christ our Lord. | Ephesians 2:8 **For by grace are ye saved through faith;** and that not of yourselves: **it is the gift of God:** |
|---|---|---|

Furthermore, the Bible tells us that the Gifts and the Calling of God are without repentance! That means that God doesn't give someone a Gift and then change His mind and take it back! God won't give someone the Free Gift of Eternal Life and then take it back from them if they have a moral failure.

> Romans 11:29 For the gifts and calling of God are without repentance.

We are also told in 2 Corinthians that Salvation will not be repented of or turned from. The context in this verse is comparing worldly sorrow to Godly sorrow. There are things in the world that will make you sorry and everyone in the world experiences sorrow at times, such as when a loved one dies. However, there is another kind of sorrow that God sends to His people that He calls to Salvation. It's the kind of sorrow that makes you realize you are lost without God and that you are a sinner. This type of sorrow results in the sinner repenting towards God and putting their trust in Jesus. The result of this sorrow is Salvation that will not be repented of! This verse tells us that true Salvation will not be turned from!

> 2 Corinthians 7:10 For godly sorrow worketh repentance to salvation **not to be repented of**: but the sorrow of the world worketh death.

The Bible also has a lot to say about Rewards. In contrast to a Gift, a Reward is worked for, and God tells us we can lose some of our Rewards! If God offers us Rewards in addition to Salvation, that should motivate us to work for them. There are some Rewards that will not be lost. For instance, Jesus says when we give a fellow believer a cup of water in His name, which means we are doing it for Him and we let the person know that, we will not lose our Reward.

Mark 9:41 For whosoever shall give you a cup of water to drink in my name, because ye belong to Christ, verily I say unto you, **he shall not lose his reward.**

Everyone who works for the Lord is going to receive some type of Reward, and we are told that the Rewards we receive will be according to our labor. In other words, Christians who work harder and accomplish more for the Kingdom can expect to receive a greater reward than those who work little.

1 Corinthians 3:8 Now he that planteth and he that watereth are one: and **every man shall receive his own reward according to his own labour.**

We are told to be diligent in our work so that we don't lose anything that we could have had. We are told we should try to receive our full reward.

2 John 1:8 Look to yourselves, that we lose not those things which we have wrought, **but that we receive a full reward**.

Jesus is going to give us our Rewards when we stand before Him at the Judgement Seat of Christ. All Christians will stand before Jesus at this Judgement Seat.

> Romans 14:10 But why dost thou judge thy brother? or why dost thou set at nought thy brother? **for we shall all stand before the judgment seat of Christ.**

It's at this Judgement Seat that the Christian will see both good things they have done in their life that benefited the Kingdom, as well as the bad things they've done. Many of us will want to hang our heads low when we see some of the stupid and selfish things we have done in the flesh, and we will wish we had done more for Jesus.

> 2 Corinthians 5:10 For we must all appear before the judgment seat of Christ; **that every one may receive the things done in his body**, according to that he hath done, whether it be good or bad.

At this time, everyone's works will be made manifest which means they will be revealed. Furthermore, they will be tried by fire to see what sore they are. This means God is going to reveal not only what we've done, but He's going to look at our intentions. For instance, if someone gives money to a church so they can get recognition, that person won't receive the reward that someone else who gives for the correct intention will receive.

> 1 Corinthians 3:13 Every man's work shall be made manifest: for the day shall declare it, because it shall be revealed by fire; and **the fire shall try every man's work of what sort it is**.

Whatever work we have that makes it through this fire will be rewarded!

---

1 Corinthians 3:14 **If any man's work abide** which he hath built thereupon, **he shall receive a reward**.

---

Some Christians will not have any work that makes it through the fire. Some will stand before Jesus and see that they wasted their lives living selfishly instead of working for the Kingdom. They'll see that everything they lived for, stressed about, and dreamed about went up in smoke because it wasn't for God's Kingdom. Nevertheless, the person will be saved even though they have nothing they've done worthy of reward!

---

1 Corinthians 3:15 <u>If any man's work shall be burned</u>, <u>he shall suffer loss</u>: **but he himself shall be saved**; yet so as by fire.

---

One might ask, what type of Rewards is God going to give to His people? We are told that we can't even imagine what God has planned for us. When we are in Eternity, what we experience will be beyond anything that's ever been seen, heard about, or thought of!

| 1 Corinthians 2:9 But as it is written, Eye hath not seen, nor ear heard, neither have entered into the heart of man, the things which God hath prepared for them that love him. | Isaiah 64:4 For since the beginning of the world men have not heard, nor perceived by the ear, neither hath the eye seen, O God, beside thee, what he hath prepared for him that waiteth for him. |

However, God does reveal to us what one type of Reward is going to be. One way in which He'll reward us is by giving us a Crown. This is the type of Crown that is worn by a King or a Queen. The Bible describes 5 different Crowns that are available and that are given as Rewards to the Believer.

The First Crown the New Testament speaks of is what some refer to as the <u>Crown of Victory</u>. The Apostle Paul tells us that he was trying to receive this Crown. This Crown only goes to a small number of Believers. What was Paul doing to try to achieve this Crown? For one, Paul didn't receive payment for his preaching of the Gospel. This doesn't mean it's wrong for a Pastor to receive a salary. As a matter of fact, the Bible supports recompensing those who work for the Lord. Paul, however, decided he'd rather make his ministry free so that all his reward would come from God, which is probably pretty smart on his part!

---

1 Corinthians 9:17 For if **I do this thing willingly, I have a reward**: but if against my will, a dispensation of the gospel is committed unto me

.

1 Corinthians 9:18 **What is my reward then**? Verily <u>that, when I preach the gospel, I may make the gospel of Christ without charge,</u> that I abuse not my power in the gospel.

---

Paul compares striving for this Crown to running a race. In his analogy, only one receives the prize. This lets us know that at most, few will receive this Crown.

---

1 Corinthians 9:24 Know ye not that they which run in a race run all, **but one receiveth the prize**? So run, that ye may obtain.

---

Paul then clarifies what the prize is. The prize is a Crown. The crown that is received in his analogy is corruptible, such as what an athlete would receive. However, the Crown he is trying to get is Incorruptible which means it will never fade or decay.

> 1 Corinthians 9:25 And every man that striveth for the mastery is temperate in all things. Now **they do it to obtain a corruptible crown; but we an incorruptible.**

Paul continues and says that he is like a runner training for a race and like a fighter who beats the air (such as a boxer shadow-boxing).

> 1 Corinthians 9:26 I therefore so run, not as uncertainly; so fight I, not as one that beateth the air:

You see, to receive this Crown you have to train yourself to deny yourself, such as when Paul didn't accept money for his preaching. The Crown of Victory goes to someone who is victorious over their fleshly desires and pleasures of this current world. Paul knew that if he didn't keep his bodily desires and lust in check, he wouldn't receive this Crown. Paul says that if he wasn't careful, he would be a castaway or rejected. Sadly, some people take this verse out of context to try to convince someone they can lose their Salvation if they don't work hard to keep it. This has nothing to do with losing Salvation. Paul is referring here to the Crown of Victory!

> 1 Corinthians 9:27 But I keep under my body, and bring it into subjection: lest that by any means, when I have preached to others, I myself should be a castaway.

The Second Crown that is spoken of is the <u>Crown of Rejoicing</u>. This Crown is also referred to as the Soul Winners Crown. The Bible says that Heaven and God Himself rejoice when a Soul is saved.

| | |
|---|---|
| Luke 15:10 Likewise, I say unto you, **there is joy in the presence of the angels of God over one sinner that repenteth.** | Zephaniah 3:17 The LORD thy God in the midst of thee is mighty; **he will save, he will rejoice over thee with joy**; he will rest in his love, he will joy over thee with singing. |

The Bible tells us it's a wise thing to win souls. Those who win souls will someday shine like the stars!

| | |
|---|---|
| Proverbs 11:30 The fruit of the righteous is a tree of life; and **he that winneth souls is wise.** | Daniel 12:3 And **they that be wise shall shine** as the brightness of the firmament; and **they that turn many to righteousness as the stars for ever and ever.** |

Paul told the Philippians that they were his crown and the Thessalonians that they were his Crown of Rejoicing.

| | |
|---|---|
| Philippians 4:1 Therefore, my brethren dearly beloved and longed for, **my joy and crown**, so stand fast in the Lord, my dearly beloved. | 1 Thessalonians 2:19 For what is our hope, or joy, **or crown of rejoicing**? Are not even ye in the presence of our Lord Jesus Christ at his coming? |

The Crown of Rejoicing will be given to those who win Souls to the Lord.

The Third Crown that we read about is the Crown of Righteousness. Jesus tells us that those who long for Righteousness are blessed.

> Matthew 5:6 Blessed are they which do hunger and thirst after righteousness: for they shall be filled.

In its current state, the Earth is full of sin and cursed. However, when Jesus returns, He is going to restore Righteousness in the Earth. In the Lord's Prayer, we are shown that we should pray for this day and desire it.

> Matthew 6:10 Thy kingdom come, **Thy will be done in earth, as it is in heaven.**

Paul told Timothy that he was going to receive a Crown of Righteousness. Paul also says that this Crown won't be given to him alone, but to all those who love the Lord's appearance.

> 2 Timothy 4:8 Henceforth there is laid up for me **a crown of righteousness**, which the Lord, the righteous judge, shall give me at that day: and not to me only, but unto all them also that love his appearing.

The Crown of Righteousness will be given to those who are longing for the Lord to return and bring Righteousness back to the Earth. It is for those who are burdened by this sinful world and can't wait for the Lord to make things right. It's not for those who want the Lord to come back someday, just not today... Rather, it's for those who hunger and thirst for Him to return.

The Fourth Crown is the <u>Crown of Life</u>. Jesus tells us that we should expect trials and tribulations in this world. We should also expect persecution for being a Christian. When people hate you and don't want to be around you because of Jesus you are Blessed!

> Luke 6:22 **Blessed are ye, when men shall hate you**, and when they shall separate you from their company, and shall reproach you, and cast out your name as evil, **for the Son of man's sake**.

How is that a blessing you may ask? If you're a true Christian and you don't go along with the World or agree with their ways, they'll hate you. The reason you're blessed is because Jesus is going to Reward you for acting like a Real Christian! Jesus has a Great Reward waiting for those who "walk the walk" rather than just "talk the talk".

> Luke 6:23 **Rejoice ye in that day, and leap for joy**: for, behold, **your reward is great in heaven:** for in the like manner did their fathers unto the prophets.

James shows us that one of the Rewards we'll receive when enduring this type of temptation is the Crown of Life. If we truly love Jesus, we'll be motivated to live for Him. The more we love Him, the less we'll care about having the world's approval, and the less we'll fear what man can do to us.

> James 1:12 Blessed is the man that endureth temptation: for **when he is tried, he shall receive the crown of life**, which the Lord hath promised to them that love him.

It's one thing to live for the Lord when there's not much persecution. It's another thing when being a Christian literally threatens your life. A lot of us have been fortunate enough to live in a place where we haven't had to face this level of persecution, but our brethren in other places have and do every day. When a person dies for the Lord's sake it's a very precious thing to Him.

| Psalm 116:15 **Precious** in the sight of the LORD **is the death of his saints.** | Psalm 72:14 He shall redeem their soul from deceit and violence: **and precious shall their blood be in his sight.** |
|---|---|

The Lord promises that those who are faithful to Him even to the point of losing their physical life, will be given the Crown of Life.

| Revelation 2:10 **Fear none of those things which thou shalt suffer:** behold, the devil shall cast some of you into prison, that ye may be tried; and ye shall have tribulation ten days: **be thou faithful unto death, and I will give thee a crown of life.** |
|---|

The Fifth Crown is the <u>Crown of Glory</u>. Jesus is our Great Shepard, but He's also given the church a local Pastor, who is also a shepherd. These men have a great responsibility to help feed the Lord's flock (His people). The Lord tells them to do their work willingly and not for money.

| 1 Peter 5:2 **Feed the flock of God** which is among you, taking the oversight thereof, not by constraint, but **willingly; not for filthy lucre**, but of a ready mind; |
|---|

They are supposed to be good examples to the flock, and they are not to lord over them, which means they don't make the flock think they are their masters or that they should serve them.

> 1 Peter 5:3 Neither as being lords over God's heritage, but being examples to the flock.

The Pastors who feed their flocks and do what the Lord requires will receive a Crown of Glory.

> 1 Peter 5:4 And when the chief Shepherd shall appear, ye shall receive a crown of glory that fadeth not away.

A Summary of the 5 Crowns.

| The Crown | Received by |
|---|---|
| The Crown of Victory | Those who deny their flesh in order to better serve the Lord |
| The Crown of Rejoicing | Those who win souls to the Lord |
| The Crown of Righteousness | Those who long for the Lord to return in Righteousness |
| The Crown of Life | Those who endure temptations and tribulation even unto death |
| The Crown of Glory | Those who shepherd the Lord's flock |

When Jesus was crucified, the soldiers placed a Crown of Thorns on His head. They mocked the One who created them by putting a purple robe on Him, which signified royalty, and by placing the crown on His head.

John 19:2 And the soldiers platted **a crown of thorns**, and put it on his head, and they put on him a purple robe,

Jesus wore a Crown of Thorns so He could give you a Crown of Gold! King David speaks of the Golden Crown. This is not a manmade crown but the Crown that the Lord will give him.

Psalm 21:1 The king shall joy in thy strength, O LORD; and in thy salvation how greatly shall he rejoice!

Psalm 21:3 For thou preventest him with the blessings of goodness: **thou settest a crown of pure gold on his head**.

None of us are worthy of a crown. Actually, there is one crown we are worthy of, which is the Crown of Thorns. Only Jesus deserves to wear a Crown of Pure Gold. The 24 Elders spoken of in Revelation realize this, and that is why they cast their crowns before the Lord.

Revelation 4:10 The four and twenty elders fall down before him that sat on the throne, and worship him that liveth for ever and ever, and **cast their crowns before the throne**, saying,

Revelation 4:11 **Thou art worthy, O Lord**, to receive glory and honour and power: for thou hast created all things, and for thy pleasure they are and were created.

When Jesus returns to Earth at the Second Coming, He's going to be wearing many Crowns. I don't know how many He'll be wearing but I think it will be at least 5!

> Revelation 19:12 His eyes were as a flame of fire, and **on his head were many crowns**; and he had a name written, that no man knew, but he himself.

Never forget that Salvation is a Free Gift from God. It can't be earned or worked for. It's not a Reward. However, also remember that there are Rewards that we should work for. If we're wise, we'll work hard to receive the Lord's Rewards. What the Lord wants to give you is far better than anything this world has to offer. Don't cheat yourself out of an Eternal Reward for some temporary pleasure. Don't let anyone take your Crown!

> Revelation 3:11 Behold, I come quickly: hold that fast which thou hast, **that no man take thy crown.**

# The Sin Unto Death

The reason there are so many different Christian denominations is that most people are not willing to study the Bible. When reading a verse that contradicts what they believe, instead of reconciling the verses, they choose which verses to believe and which to ignore. Every Denomination can show you Bible verses that seem to confirm their beliefs. However, the only way to understand the Bible properly is to follow its instructions. God tells us that to understand His Doctrine, precept must be upon precept, and line upon line, here a little and there a little. This means when you read a precept in Genesis, that precept will hold true in Revelation. It is here a little and there a little. A little in Deuteronomy, a little in Romans, a little in Exodus, and a little in John.

Isaiah 28:9 **Whom shall he teach knowledge? and whom shall he make to understand doctrine**? them that are weaned from the milk, and drawn from the breasts.

Isaiah 28:10 For **precept must be upon precept**, precept upon precept; **line upon line**, line upon line; **here a little, and there a little**:

An example of precept upon precept is in the Gospel message itself. We see a precept in Genesis that shows us that when we sin, we die. That precept doesn't change anywhere in the Bible. We also see a precept in Genesis that God will provide a covering for sin. When Jesus died for our sins, He wasn't changing the precept. You see, Jesus took our place and died for us. Another precept that is learned in Genesis is that God accepts a Sacrifice for sin and Jesus was sacrificed for us. In the story of Abraham, we have a precept that shows us that God is willing to declare a person to be Righteous through Faith. Abraham was counted Righteous because he Trusted in the Lord and not because of any works he did.

The Bible is clear from Genesis to Revelation that Salvation is a Gift that is given through Faith apart from works. If that precept is not established in your heart, you may misinterpret several passages in the Bible. Also, you may come to believe that Salvation is achieved by being a good person, or you may think that while the death of Jesus was required as payment for your sins, it wasn't totally sufficient and that you must also contribute to your Salvation through your works and obedience. That belief is a false gospel.

A common passage in the Bible that is misinterpreted is in regard to the "Sin Unto Death". Some believe that God will have mercy on certain sins but that He will not have mercy on other sins. In other words, they think a Christian can commit lesser sins and still maintain their Salvation, but if they commit some greater sin (which is not defined by John) they could lose their Salvation.

> 1 John 5:16 If any man see his brother sin a sin which is not unto death, he shall ask, and he shall give him life for them that sin not unto death. **There is a sin unto death: I do not say that he shall pray for it.**

The question we must ask is, what sin is the Apostle John referring to? If there is a sin that could cause a Christian to lose their Salvation, don't you think John should have helped us out and told us what it was?? Furthermore, John says we shouldn't pray for someone who is committing this sin. If we don't know what sin the "Sin Unto Death" is, then how would we know whether or not we should pray for it??

Luckily, the Bible defines the Sin Unto Death for us. Shortly before the Jews were conquered by Babylon, God told Jeremiah not to pray for them! He told Jeremiah that if he prayed for them, He would not hear him!

> Jeremiah 7:16 Therefore **pray not thou for this people**, neither lift up cry nor prayer for them, neither make intercession to me: **for I will not hear thee**.

God explains why he told Jeremiah not to pray for them. He tells Jeremiah that He had spoken to them, but they wouldn't listen, and even after sending them many prophets they still refused to listen to Him.

> Jeremiah 7:24 But **they hearkened not**, nor inclined their ear, but walked in the counsels and in the imagination of their evil heart, and went backward, and not forward.
>
> Jeremiah 7:25 Since the day that your fathers came forth out of the land of Egypt unto this day **I have even sent unto you all my servants the prophets**, daily rising up early and sending them:

Then God tells Jeremiah, that even though he is going to also prophesy to them, they are not going to listen to Jeremiah either.

> Jeremiah 7:27 Therefore **thou shalt speak all these words unto them; but they will not hearken to thee**: thou shalt also call unto them; but they will not answer thee.

Jeremiah continued to prophesy to the Jews and tell them everything that the Lord commanded him to say. However, once again God tells Jeremiah not to pray for them.

> Jeremiah 11:14 **Therefore pray not thou for this people**, neither lift up a cry or prayer for them: for I will not hear them in the time that they cry unto me for their trouble.

Once again, God explains why Jeremiah is not to pray for them. He tells Jeremiah that He has spoken and protested to them, telling them to obey Him and not to follow other gods.

> Jeremiah 11:7 **For I earnestly protested unto your fathers** in the day that I brought them up out of the land of Egypt, even unto this day, **rising early and protesting, saying, Obey my voice.**

But even though the Lord spoke to them, they refused to hear Him.

> Jeremiah 11:10 They are turned back to the iniquities of their forefathers, **which refused to hear my words**; and they went after other gods to serve them: the house of Israel and the house of Judah have broken my covenant which I made with their fathers.

The reason that God told Jeremiah not to pray for the Jews is because He had clearly spoken to them and made His voice clear. You see, they understood the message. They had a clear understanding of what God's message was and yet they refused to listen! God wasn't going to force them to obey. They had to obey by their own free will.

Before we continue, we must understand something. Going to Church doesn't make anyone a Christian or a true believer. From the early days of the Church, there were false prophets and there were people in the Church who thought they were saved but were not. When the Apostles wrote letters to the churches they addressed the true church, but they also included warnings to those in the church who were not truly saved. Don't get caught up in the notion that because an apostle addresses a letter to the church, everything written applies to the true Born-Again believer because it doesn't. There are many in the church who are called Brothers or Sisters, but they are not true believers and Paul tells us not to have fellowship with these types of people.

> 1 Corinthians 5:11 But now I have written unto you not to keep company, **if any man that is called a brother** be a fornicator, or covetous, or an idolator, or a railer, or a drunkard, or an extortioner; with such an one no not to eat.

James shows us that there are people in the church who are called brethren who don't believe the truth and that by converting them, we assist in saving their souls! James is not referring to the truth of non-salvific issues such as whether the rapture is pre or post-trib. He is referring to the truth of the Gospel.

> James 5:19 **Brethren, if any of you do err from the truth**, and one convert him;
>
> James 5:20 Let him know, that **he which converteth the sinner from the error of his way shall save a soul from death**, and shall hide a multitude of sins.

The Apostles started churches, set up leaders in the local church, and then moved on to start other churches. They knew that after they left, false believers would come in, and false pastors whom they referred to as Wolves. Paul warned the Ephesians of these Wolves.

> Acts 20:29 For I know this, that after my departing shall grievous **wolves** enter in among you, not sparing the flock.

Peter and Jude both wrote about these Wolves in detail. Both Peter and Jude say that these Wolves are in ministry for money and compare them to Balaam from the Old Testament who was hired by the enemies of God to try to curse His people.

| 2 Peter 2:15 Which have forsaken the right way, and are gone astray, **following the way of Balaam the son of Bosor, who loved the wages of unrighteousness;** | Jude 11 Woe unto them! for they have gone in the way of Cain, and **ran greedily after the error of Balaam for reward,** and perished in the gainsaying of Core. |
|---|---|

Peter and Jude both make it clear that these are unsaved individuals.

| 2 Peter 2:17 **These are wells without water**, clouds that are carried with a tempest; to whom the mist of darkness is reserved for ever. | Jude 19 **These be they** who separate themselves, sensual, **having not the Spirit**. |
|---|---|

The Wolves deny Jesus and the True Gospel.

| 2 Peter 2:1 But there were false prophets also among the people, even as there shall be false teachers among you, **who privily shall bring in damnable heresies, even denying the Lord that bought them**, and bring upon themselves swift destruction. | Jude 4 For there are certain men crept in unawares, who were before of old ordained to this condemnation, ungodly men, turning the grace of our God into lasciviousness, **and denying the only Lord God, and our Lord Jesus Christ.** |

The Wolves speak evil of the True Gospel, and they have many followers.

| 2 Peter 2:2 And many shall follow their pernicious ways; **by reason of whom the way of truth shall be evil spoken of.** |

They lure people who have escaped from others living in error. For example, they lure someone who may have been hooked on drugs out of that lifestyle and promise them freedom and salvation.

| 2 Peter 2:18 For when they speak great swelling words of vanity, **they allure** through the lusts of the flesh, through much wantonness, those that were clean escaped from them who live in error. |

However, while the Wolves promise freedom, they themselves are servants of Satan and of destruction.

| 2 Peter 2:19 **While they promise them liberty, they themselves are the servants of corruption**: for of whom a man is overcome, of the same is he brought in bondage. |

Peter then tells us that these people who follow the Wolves are in a worse condition than if they'd never heard about Jesus!

> 2 Peter 2:20 For if after they have escaped the pollutions of the world through the knowledge of the Lord and Saviour Jesus Christ, they are again entangled therein, and overcome, **the latter end is worse with them than the beginning.**

You see, the Wolves claim to preach the correct gospel and they are very persuasive. However, the gospel they preach is False and will not save souls. The Wolf is mostly concerned with getting people's money. Because of that, they will focus mostly on prosperity and trying to link all of God's Blessings to tithing and giving. Of course, the Wolf takes the money for themselves, and in extreme cases, spends it on their lust such as multimillion-dollar homes and private jets. Peter goes on to explain that these people are turning from the Holy Commandment.

> 2 Peter 2:21 For it had been better for them not to have known the way of righteousness, than, after they have known it, **to turn from the holy commandment delivered unto them.**

What Holy Commandment are they turning from? They are turning from the Holy Commandment to Trust Jesus and Believe in Him alone for Salvation. This contradicts the Wolf's message which usually involves works for Salvation and denies the power of the New Birth.

> 1 John 3:23 And **this is his commandment, That we should believe on the name of his Son Jesus Christ**, and love one another, as he gave us commandment.

It's a dangerous thing to have a Holy Bible and to go to church all your life and not be Born Again! It's not that these people lost their Salvation. The problem is that instead of listening to God's Word, they listened to the Wolf instead. Why would they listen to the Wolf and trust what the Wolf says instead of the True Gospel? The Bible says the Wolves deceive the hearts of the Simple.

> Romans 16:18 For they that are such serve not our Lord Jesus Christ, but their own belly; and **by good words and fair speeches deceive the hearts of the simple.**

Who are the Simple? The Bible defines who the Simple is. The Simple are those who believe what the Wolf tells them without searching the matter out. Instead of reading their Bible to see if what the Wolf is saying is true, they blindly follow what the Wolf says.

> Proverbs 14:15 **The simple believeth every word**: but the prudent man looketh well to his going.

The people who follow the Wolves are like dogs and pigs. You can put clothes on a dog but it's still a dog. You can wash a pig and put a dress and lipstick on it to make it look pretty, but the pig will still jump in a mud puddle because it's a pig! Dogs and Pigs are unclean animals and do what they do because of their nature. These people never had a change of Nature.

> 2 Peter 2:22 But it is happened unto them according to the true proverb, **The dog is turned to his own vomit again; and the sow that was washed to her wallowing in the mire.**

Someone who is truly Born-Again has a new Nature. The New Nature is given to us by God when we're saved and it's Him that gives us the power to live Holy. We're not pigs and dogs that have been given a bath, but we are new creatures who partake in God's Holy Nature!

---

2 Peter 1:3 According as **his divine power hath given unto us all things that pertain unto life and godliness**, through the knowledge of him that hath called us to glory and virtue:

2 Peter 1:4 Whereby are given unto us exceeding great and precious promises: that by these **ye might be partakers of the divine nature**, having escaped the corruption that is in the world through lust.

---

So, what is the Sin Unto Death? The Sin Unto Death is turning away from God's message of Salvation after having a clear understanding of it. Most people don't understand the Gospel, even people who've been in church all their lives. When we realize someone who is called a brother or sister is not following the truth, we are supposed to present the True Gospel to them and try to help them understand it. If they don't understand it, we should pray for God to help them understand. This applies to someone outside the church as well.

However, if the issue is not that they don't understand, but rather they understand but simply reject the message, then we shouldn't pray for God to make them Trust in Him. God will not violate someone's free will and make them put their Trust in Him. He won't flip a switch in their hearts and cause them to believe. I've prayed many times for God to make someone believe the Gospel, and most of us with lost loved ones will do this.

However, we must realize that if God flipped a switch in our loved one's hearts and made them believe, then He'd be obligated to flip everyone's switch and make everyone believe, and He simply will not do that. He gives everyone the choice to put their Trust in Him. He gives us free will and wants us to willingly choose to Believe and Trust Him. He wants a real loving relationship and not something that is forced upon someone.

I told you it's a dangerous thing to have a Holy Bible and to go to church and not be Born Again. God will hold a person who has access to the truth much more accountable on judgment day than someone who didn't have much access to it. We must make our calling and election sure. We must make sure we understand the true Gospel and follow it, and that we don't blindly follow a Wolf. When a person understands God's message and the Gospel of Jesus Christ but turns from it, they will remain in the Congregation of the Dead. Instead of the Dead Person being Born-Again and given Life, the Dead remains with the Dead.

Proverbs 21:16 The man that wandereth out of the way of understanding **shall remain in the congregation of the dead**.

They don't leave the Congregation of the Living because they were never a part of that Congregation. Rather, they remain where they are, which is with the Dead. This is the Sin Unto Death.

# Preserved by the Lord

If the Lord forgave us of all our past sins and mistakes, that alone would be a great mercy. It's a great kindness to give someone a second chance. King David realized that God had shown him mercy and that He had saved his soul from Hell.

> Psalm 86:13 For great is thy mercy toward me: and thou hast delivered my soul from the lowest hell.

However, our problem is that as long as we're still in a body of flesh and blood, we're not perfect. We still have some magnitude of sin in our lives even after being Born Again. If it were up to us to keep ourselves saved, we wouldn't remain saved for one day! So, we need the Lord to not only save us from our past sins, but we need Him to preserve us, and to keep us in relationship with Him. King David realized this, and He asked God if He would keep him saved.

> Psalm 56:13 <u>For thou hast delivered my soul from death</u>: **wilt not thou deliver my feet from falling**, that I may walk before God in the light of the living?

Now, Hannah who was the Prophet Samuel's mother, had previously had a revelation. Hannah said that God would keep the feet of His saints. She also made a statement that by strength a man would not prevail. What Hannah was saying is that a man could not find or keep Salvation in his own power.

1 Samuel 2:9 **He will keep the feet of his saints**, and the wicked shall be silent in darkness; for **by strength shall no man prevail**.

God continued to speak to David and revealed to him that He would hold David's hand. This means that God is going to be with David and is going to be always holding on to him.

Psalm 73:23 Nevertheless I am continually with thee: **thou hast holden me by my right hand.**

God has promised to hold our hand as well.

Isaiah 41:13 For I the LORD thy God **will hold thy right hand**, saying unto thee, Fear not; **I will help thee**.

This didn't mean that David would never fall. He would fall at times. However, because God is holding David's hand, he would not be utterly cast down.

Psalm 37:24 Though he fall, he shall not be utterly cast down: **for the LORD upholdeth him with his hand.**

David knew that the Lord would uphold others as well. He knew this grace would not only be extended to him but to all those who belonged to the Lord.

> Psalm 145:14 **The LORD upholdeth all that fall**, and raiseth up all those that be bowed down.

A Just Man (a person declared righteous by the Lord) may fall many times. However, because God is holding our hand, we'll get back up!

> Proverbs 24:16 **For a just man falleth seven times, and riseth up again**: but the wicked shall fall into mischief.

By the time David wrote Psalm 116, he had received the answer he was looking for. He knew that God was going to keep him.

| Psalm 56:13 For thou hast delivered my soul from death: **wilt not thou deliver my feet from falling**, that I may walk before God in the light of the living? | Psalm 116:8 For thou hast delivered my soul from death, mine eyes from tears, **and my feet from falling**. |
|---|---|

It was the Lord who preserved David and kept him. David wasn't keeping himself in his own power. The Lord held David's hand and didn't let him go. The Lord Jesus told us that when He holds our hand, no one will pluck us away or out of His Hand. Once He has you, He intends to hang on!

> John 10:28 **And I give unto them eternal life; and they shall never perish**, neither shall any man pluck them out of my hand.
>
> John 10:29 My Father, which gave them me, is greater than all; and **no man is able to pluck them out of my Father's hand**.

When Jesus saves us, He begins working on us and through us! Remember, the Holy Ghost is inside of us giving us Life and Renewing us. Salvation is not a past experience but an ongoing work of the Lord. The good news is that when you're Born Again and the Lord starts His work on you, He's going to finish it!

> Philippians 1:6 Being confident of this very thing, that **he which hath begun a good work in you will perform it until the day of Jesus Christ**:

It's the Lord who is performing the work, not us. The Lord Jesus is our Advocate and High Priest. Because of Him, we are blameless in the eyes of God. We're promised that He will confirm us unto the end.

> 1 Corinthians 1:8 **Who shall also confirm you unto the end**, that ye may be blameless in the day of our Lord Jesus Christ.

When we arrive at the end, God will say we are unblameable and holy!

> 1 Thessalonians 3:13 **To the end he may stablish your hearts unblameable in holiness before God**, even our Father, at the coming of our Lord Jesus Christ with all his saints.

The reason God will call us Holy and unblameable is because our sins are covered by the Blood of Jesus. He has given us Christ's Righteousness; therefore, a sinner is seen as a saint who has no sin!

> Colossians 1:22 <u>In the body of his flesh through death,</u> **to present you holy and unblameable and unreproveable in his sight:**

The Lord is at work right now preserving us. Remember, He promised in Isaiah that He would hold our hand. He is Faithful to do what He says!

> 1 Thessalonians 5:23 And the very God of peace sanctify you wholly; and I pray God your whole spirit and soul and body **be preserved blameless unto the coming of our Lord Jesus Christ.**
>
> 1 Thessalonians 5:24 **Faithful is he that calleth you, who also will do it.**

The Lord is able and has promised to Preserve us. It is Him that keeps our feet from falling. Though we may fall temporarily, He holds us in His Hand and pulls us back up.

| Psalm 116:8 For thou hast delivered my soul from death, mine eyes from tears, **and my feet from falling.** | Jude 24 **Now unto him that is able to keep you from falling,** and to present you faultless before the presence of his glory with exceeding joy, |
|---|---|

God foresees all those who will Believe in Him and come to Salvation.  In other words, He knows what's going to happen before it happens.  God calls those people to Himself through Faith in Jesus.  When we Trust in Jesus and are born-again, we are given to Jesus and become Children of Christ or Children of the Lord.  We are promised that the Lord will never cast us away when this happens!

> John 6:37 All that the Father giveth me shall come to me; and him that cometh to me I will in no wise cast out.

Jesus tells us that He was sent to accomplish the Father's will.

> John 6:38 For I came down from heaven, not to do mine own will, but the will of him that sent me.

Jesus then tells us that it's the will of the Father that Jesus will not lose anyone who the Father has given Him!  Moreover, not only will Jesus not lose anyone who was given to Him, but He will raise them up on the last day, which is the last day of the current age of time we're living in.  Notice, Jesus is the One who is accomplishing this.  This isn't us hanging on to Jesus, but it's Jesus hanging on to us and carrying us through to the end!  If any truly Born-Again person were to lose their salvation, then Jesus would fail in accomplishing the Father's will.  Of course, that won't happen, and Jesus will perform the will of the Father!

> John 6:39 And **this is the Father's will** which hath sent me, that of all which he hath given me **I should lose nothing,** but should raise it up again at the last day.

It's God's Power that saves us and keeps us saved. God promised to do this in the Old Testament as well as the New Testament. Jesus prayed that the Father would keep those given to Him through His own name. The entire Godhead is active in keeping us saved!

John 17:11 And now I am no more in the world, but these are in the world, and I come to thee. **Holy Father, keep through thine own name those whom thou hast given me**, that they may be one, as we are.

The Father answered the prayer of the Son, and He keeps all those who belong to Him. Peter realized that we are kept by the Power of God.

1 Peter 1:5 **Who are kept by the power of God** through faith unto salvation ready to be revealed in the last time.

God is going to preserve His saints forever. To preserve something is to keep it from spoiling or free from decay. It also means to keep something alive. It means to keep something from perishing. Those who have been Born Again will Never Perish. We are Preserved Forever!

Psalm 37:28 For the LORD loveth judgment, and forsaketh not **his saints; they are preserved for ever**: but the seed of the wicked shall be cut off.

# What God does will last Forever

Salvation is a complete work of God. It's God who saves us and keeps us saved. Someone who is Born-Again doesn't get saved through any act of themselves. The Bible says we are not born of blood which means we aren't born again through our bloodline, such as being Jewish etc. We are not born again through the will of the flesh, which means we can't decide in our flesh that we're going to be saved, and then perform some work such as walking an aisle or being water baptized. Also, we are not born again through the will of man, which among other things means that no one can pray you into Heaven or into a saved condition. The Bible says we are Born-Again through the will of God, which means Salvation is a work that God alone does.

> John 1:13 **Which were born,** not of blood, nor of the will of the flesh, nor of the will of man, but **of God**.

The Apostle James tells us that God begat us, which means born us unto Himself, through the Word of Truth. The Word of Truth is the Gospel of Jesus. It's by Trusting in Jesus that we are saved and it's God who initiates this and begets us. We are Born Again as His children entirely by His power.

James 1:18 **Of his own will begat he us with the word of truth**, that we should be a kind of firstfruits of his creatures.

When God saves us, He places a seed in our hearts which grows and produces fruit. It also grows into a "New Man" and a new creature. The seed that takes root in our hearts is the Gospel message and is the Word of God. Jesus reveals to us that the seed is the Word of God.

Luke 8:11 Now the parable is this: **The seed is the word of God**.

When we are born into this world we are born of a corruptible seed. We are born of flesh and blood, and because we sin, we eventually perish and die. However, when we are Born of God, we are born of an incorruptible seed! This means that the "New Man" which is our born-again spirit man, cannot be corrupted!

1 Peter 1:23 **Being born again, not of corruptible seed, but of incorruptible**, by the word of God, which liveth and abideth for ever.

Peter shows us that the old man who is born of the corruptible seed will perish and wither away just like grass does. This is our flesh.

> 1 Peter 1:24 For **all flesh is as grass,** and all the glory of man as the flower of grass. **The grass withereth**, and the flower thereof falleth away:

However, the Word of the Lord, which is the incorruptible seed, will never perish. This means the "New Man" can never perish because he is born from that seed!

| 1 Peter 1:25 But **the word of the Lord endureth for ever**. And this is **the word which by the gospel** is preached unto you. | Isaiah 40:8 <u>The grass withereth, the flower fadeth</u>: but **the word of our God shall stand for ever.** |
|---|---|

Remember that after we are Born Again, we must still struggle in our Flesh as long as we are in our natural bodies. The Flesh is our Old Man. The Old Man is corrupt because he is born of the corruptible seed. The Apostle Paul shows us that we need to stop listening to the "Old Man".

> Ephesians 4:22 That ye **put off** concerning the former conversation **the old man, which is corrupt** according to the deceitful lusts;

We should be renewed in our minds by the spirit of our new man.

> Ephesians 4:23 And be renewed in the spirit of your mind;

We do this by putting on the New Man, or in other words walking in the Spirit. When we live our lives focusing on the Lord and His Word and listening to His voice, we are putting on the New Man and walking in the Spirit. Now, notice the New Man is created by God and is righteous and holy!

Ephesians 4:24 And that ye put on **the new man**, which after God **is created in righteousness and true holiness.**

The Apostle John shows us that the New Man cannot sin! The reason the New Man cannot sin is because he is created from the incorruptible seed and the seed remains in him! The New Man is born of God and is not capable of sinning!

1 John 3:9 Whosoever is born of God doth not commit sin; for **his seed remaineth in him**: and he cannot sin, because he is born of God.

Am I saying that a Born-Again Christian can't sin? No! Remember, we have a dual nature. We have an Old Man, and we have a New Man. In our flesh we still sin at times, however, the New Man who is our born-again spirit doesn't sin. This is why Paul said that when he sinned it wasn't him that was sinning but sin that dwelled in him. He is referring to the sin that is in his flesh or in his Old Man.

Romans 7:17 Now then **it is no more I that do it**, but sin that dwelleth in me.

Romans 7:20 Now if I do that I would not, it is no more I that do it, **but sin that dwelleth in me**.

Paul shows us that the New Man delights in God's Law. The Inward Man that Paul refers to is the same as the New Man which is the Born-Again spiritual man.

> Romans 7:22 For I delight in the law of God after the inward man:

Paul understands that his Old Man will always be a servant to sin. You will never fully conquer sin in your flesh. However, the New Man that is created by God through the incorruptible seed, serves God and His Law.

> Romans 7:25 I thank God through Jesus Christ our Lord. So then **with the mind I myself serve the law of God**; but with the flesh the law of sin.

Satan can touch and afflict the Old Man. Because of our sin, our flesh is subject to decay, and it dies. However, we are promised that the New Man will not be touched by that wicked one! Our New Man is Born of God and does not sin! The Spirit of the Born Again person does not sin but keeps itself through the power of God.

> 1 John 5:18 We know that **whosoever is born of God** sinneth not; but **he that is begotten of God keepeth himself,** and that wicked one toucheth him not.

Jesus is the only One who was sinless in the flesh. When Jesus lived His life free from sin, He overcame the power of Satan and of the world.

> John 16:33 These things I have spoken unto you, that in me ye might have peace. In the world ye shall have tribulation: but be of good cheer; **I have overcome the world.**

The Bible tells us that whoever is Born Again also overcomes the world thru faith in Jesus.

> 1 John 5:4 For **whatsoever is born of God overcometh the world**: and this is **the victory that overcometh the world, even our faith**.

False Religion which includes many who call themselves Christians, try to get the Old Man good enough to make it to Heaven. This is sad because they'll never get the Old Man to be good enough. They don't realize that you must be perfect to get to Heaven. We are Perfect in Jesus. It's our New Man who is saved and going to glory. The Old Man which is our flesh and blood cannot inherit God's Kingdom.

> 1 Corinthians 15:50 Now this I say, brethren, that **flesh and blood cannot inherit the kingdom of God**; neither doth corruption inherit incorruption.

Salvation is an act of God! It will last forever. It's God who begets us and by whom we are Born-Again. We are Born Again through God's incorruptible seed. Nothing can be added to it, and nothing can be taken away from it. The New Man will NEVER die!

> Ecclesiastes 3:14 I know that, **whatsoever God doeth, it shall be for ever**: nothing can be put to it, nor any thing taken from it: and God doeth it, that men should fear before him.

# The Lord Knows Those Who Are His

Before God created the world, He foreknew those who would put their Trust in Him. In other words, God knew before you were born whether your heart would be willing to Trust Him and to Believe the Gospel. God knows who belongs to Him and who is playing religion. So, as He says in Nahum, He knows those who Trust in Him.

> Nahum 1:7 The LORD is good, a strong hold in the day of trouble; and **he knoweth them that trust in him**.

When the Lord speaks of knowing someone, He isn't just referring to the fact that He has knowledge of them. To know the Lord and for the Lord to know you means He has a personal relationship with you. All Born Again Christians have a personal relationship with the Lord. Many people think they are saved and know the Lord through their religion. Sadly, if there's no personal relationship, the Lord will someday tell them "I Never Knew You".

In the Old Covenant, the knowledge of God was taught by men from generation to generation. Moses delivered the law to Israel, and they were to teach it to their children. Those who took the law to heart would have a mark so to speak which would identify them. This sign or mark would be in their hands which indicates a person's work or actions, and it would be in their forehead, between their eyes, which would indicate that it directed their vision or focus.

Deuteronomy 6:7 And **thou shalt teach them diligently** unto thy children, and shalt talk of them when thou sittest in thine house, and when thou walkest by the way, and when thou liest down, and when thou risest up.

Deuteronomy 6:8 And thou shalt bind them for **a sign upon thine hand**, and they shall be **as frontlets between thine eyes**.

The problem Israel had with the Old Covenant was that keeping the Covenant relied upon the strength of the flesh. In order to know God and have a relationship with Him, Israel had to keep His laws. Joshua and the people who entered the Promised Land served the Lord during Joshua's life. However, in one generation, Israel went from serving the Lord to not Knowing Him.

Judges 2:10 And also all that generation were gathered unto their fathers: and there arose another generation after them, **which knew not the LORD**, nor yet the works which he had done for Israel.

During the time of the Judges, Israel had trouble after trouble. It seemed like the Covenant was hanging by a tread because the Lord would raise up a Judge who would help Israel get back on the right track, but then they would fall away again and again. They would stop trusting in the Lord and follow other gods. It wasn't until the days of David that Israel seemed to wholly follow the Lord. David trusted the Lord and had a personal relationship with Him, and he led Israel to trust in and follow the Lord. David said that those who know the Lord and trust Him are God's people and His sheep.

> Psalm 100:3 Know ye that the LORD he is God: it is he that hath made us, and not we ourselves; **we are his people, and the sheep of his pasture.**

After David died, Israel fell away again. It seemed like things were going well, and they were, under the rule of Solomon. However, Solomon committed acts of idolatry in order to please his wives and this eventually led to the Kingdom of Israel being split. Eventually, God had enough, and hundreds of years later the Kingdom was lost. Still, God had a remnant of people who trusted in Him and had a relationship with Him after the manner of David and Abraham, which was based on Faith. So, God promised that He was going to establish a New Covenant with Israel. However, unlike the Old Covenant, knowing God would not rely on the strength of the flesh. God promised that everyone who was a part of this Covenant was going to Know Him! From the least to the greatest says God.

| | |
|---|---|
| Jeremiah 31:34 And **they shall teach no more** every man his neighbour, and every man his brother, saying, **Know the LORD: for they shall all know me, from the least of them unto the greatest of them,** saith the LORD: for I will forgive their iniquity, and I will remember their sin no more. | Hebrews 8:11 And they shall not teach every man his neighbour, and every man his brother, saying, **Know the Lord: for all shall know me, from the least to the greatest.** |

Remember, David said that God's people are His sheep. Jesus tells us that when we Trust in Him, we are His sheep. Furthermore, Jesus tells us that when we are His sheep, we will Know Him and He will Know us!

> John 10:14 I am the good shepherd, and **know my sheep**, and **am known of mine.**

Those who are the Lord's sheep hear His voice and they follow Him.

> John 10:27 My sheep hear my voice, **and I know them**, and **they follow me:**

When someone Trusts in the Lord, God puts a mark upon them. Ezekial had a vision, and in the vision, God said to put a mark on the forehead of everyone who mourned for the evil things going on in Jerusalem at the time.

> Ezekiel 9:4 And the LORD said unto him, Go through the midst of the city, through the midst of Jerusalem, and **set a mark upon the foreheads of the men that sigh and that cry** for all the abominations that be done in the midst thereof.

As I said, this was a vision. However, it is a picture of what God does and how He marks those who Trust in Him. The mark is not physical or at least something we can see with the physical eye, but I believe it's something that angels and demons can see. The mark lets angelic powers know they need to spare the person from wrath among other things. Another example of this is found in Revelation, where the angels are told to seal the 144,000 in their foreheads before they begin to pour out wrath on the earth.

> Revelation 7:3 Saying, Hurt not the earth, neither the sea, nor the trees, **till we have sealed the servants of our God in their foreheads**.

Satan will often try to mimic God. During the Tribulation, Satan will also mark people in their hands and foreheads. This is famously known as the Mark of the Beast and will be instituted at the time of the Antichrist. We don't know for sure, but it seems that this mark will be physical and be able to be seen by men because it will dictate whether people can buy or sell. This is Satan's imitation of God's mark.

> Revelation 13:16 And he causeth all, both small and great, rich and poor, free and bond, **to receive a mark in their right hand, or in their foreheads:**

The Mark of the Beast will be the name of the Beast or Antichrist, or at least it will signify his name. Eventually, everyone is going to have one of two names on their foreheads, either Satan's name or God's.

We're shown that the seal whereby the 144,000 are sealed is the name of God.

> Revelation 14:1 And I looked, and, lo, a Lamb stood on the mount Sion, and with him an hundred forty and four thousand, **having his Father's name written in their foreheads.**

We're also shown that all the citizens of New Jerusalem will have our Father's name in our foreheads as well, so this isn't something exclusive to the 144,000!

> Revelation 22:4 And they shall see his face; and **his name shall be in their foreheads.**

The Bible shows us that all Born Again Believers are sealed. I used to think of this seal as the type of seal that would be on a jar. I would hope that nothing strong enough to pop the seal would come along. However, that's not the type of seal the Bible is referring to. The type of seal the Bible is referring to is a stamp or a mark of approval, and it's what a king would use. Kings would use this type of seal to certify something was from them and had their approval. It would ensure that the thing sealed got to its destination without being tampered with.

| John 3:33 He that hath received his testimony hath **set to his seal** that God is true. | The person who believes the Gospel "sets to their seal" that God is true. This means the person certifies or gives their "Stamp of Approval" on God's message. |
|---|---|

The Bible tells us that when we put our Trust in the Gospel we are sealed with the Holy Spirit! I used to think this read "sealed by the Holy Spirit". However, it's not by but with. In other words, the Seal is the Holy Spirit Himself! The Holy Spirit is God's Stamp of Approval on the Believer.

> Ephesians 1:13 <u>In whom ye also trusted</u>, after that ye heard the word of truth, <u>the gospel of your salvation</u>: in whom also <u>after that ye believed</u>, **ye were sealed with that holy Spirit of promise,**

God marks or stamps the Believer with The Holy Spirit, which is His Seal of Approval. The Seal, which is the Holy Spirit, is our earnest or downpayment that God has placed upon us. God purchased our souls with His blood on the cross. An earnest payment is something that a buyer gives as a good faith deposit, which shows his intention to complete the purchase. God gives us His Holy Spirit as an earnest deposit which shows us that He intends to complete the deal, which is our total redemption.

> Ephesians 1:14 **Which is the earnest** of our inheritance **until the redemption of the purchased possession**, unto the praise of his glory.

One of the New Covenant promises is that God will put His fear into the hearts of His believers. This fear will prevent the believer from departing from Him. This is not a maybe, it is a New Covenant fact and a promise from God.

> Jeremiah 32:40 And I will make an everlasting covenant with them, that I will not turn away from them, to do them good; but **I will put my fear in their hearts, that they shall not depart from me.**

Among other things, this is one of the reasons that the Apostle John knew that those who had departed the faith were never really part of the true church. They were never truly Born Again.

> 1 John 2:19 They went out from us, but they were not of us; for **if they had been of us, they would no doubt have continued with us**: but they went out, that they might be made manifest that they were not all of us.

The New Testament scriptures explain how God keeps us from departing from Him. We know He puts His fear in us, but He explains this in further detail in the Epistles. First, we are told that God anoints us with the Holy Spirit. God anoints and seals us with His Holy Spirit.

> 2 Corinthians 1:21 Now he which stablisheth us with you in Christ, **and hath anointed us**, is God;
>
> 2 Corinthians 1:22 **Who hath also sealed us**, and given the earnest of the Spirit in our hearts.

We are then told that the anointing we receive, which is the Holy Spirit, remains in us and teaches us. He leads us into truth in all things. He also teaches and causes us to remain in the faith, and to abide in Jesus. Because of the work of the Holy Spirit, we shall abide in Jesus. Not that we could or should, but we shall, or in other words Will!

> 1 John 2:27 But **the anointing which ye have received of him abideth in you**, and ye need not that any man teach you: but as the same anointing teacheth you of all things, and is truth, and is no lie, and **even as it hath taught you, ye shall abide in him.**

Jesus told us that when the Comforter comes to us, which is the Holy Spirit also called the Holy Ghost, He will abide with us forever. We will know Him and He will be with us and in us.

> John 14:16 And I will pray the Father, and he shall give you another Comforter, that **he may abide with you for ever**;
>
> John 14:17 Even the Spirit of truth; whom the world cannot receive, because it seeth him not, neither knoweth him: **but ye know him**; for he dwelleth with you, and shall be in you.

But what if we sin, you may ask? How can the Holy Spirit remain with us when we fall short and sin. The Bible says that it grieves the Holy Spirit when we sin. Although it causes Him grief, He suffers through it and remains with us, because God has sealed us unto the day of redemption. Note, He doesn't say until, He says unto. The reason it's important to make that distinction is because God has made His Seal to be Unto Redemption. In other words, the Seal will not and cannot be broken! The Holy Spirit will carry the Believer to Redemption and Nothing will stop Him from accomplishing His purpose!

> Ephesians 4:30 <u>And grieve not the holy Spirit of God</u>, whereby **ye are sealed unto the day of redemption.**

True Born-Again Believers are eternally Sealed by God. He has anointed us with His Holy Spirit. I believe when the Father looks at us, He sees the name of Jesus in our foreheads. Those who receive the Mark of the Beast will be eternally damned. Those who receive the Mark of the Lamb will be Eternally Saved!

Sometimes this can be hard to believe. We see so many people who were once religious and seemed to be Christians who fall away. If you're not careful this can make you doubt some of the promises of God. Paul and Timothy were dealing with this in their day. Paul warned Timothy about a couple of Heretics in the church who were overthrowing some of the church member's faith. In other words, these two guys were preaching false doctrine and as a result, people were leaving the faith or leaving Jesus.

> 2 Timothy 2:17 And their word will eat as doth a canker: of whom is Hymenaeus and Philetus;
>
> 2 Timothy 2:18 Who concerning the truth have erred, saying that the resurrection is past already; **and overthrow the faith of some**.

However, Paul encourages Timothy and tells him that God's word is sure, in other words certain. Moreover, God's word has a seal or statement that says: The Lord Knows Those Who Are His! Some will fall away, however those who the Lord knows will remain with Him! This was an encouragement to Timothy, and it should be an encouragement to us as well. When the Lord saves you and places His deposit on you, you can be assured He's going to complete the deal!

> 2 Timothy 2:19 Nevertheless <u>the foundation of God standeth sure, having this seal</u>, **The Lord knoweth them that are his**. And, let every one that nameth the name of Christ depart from iniquity.

# The Everlasting Covenant

They say that if something sounds too good to be true, it probably is. There is in fact a lot of wisdom to that statement and generally, you would be wise to follow that precept. On the other hand, a few things are "So Good That They Must Be True". The Gospel of Salvation is so good that it must be true because no sinful man could have invented that message. They say that nothing lasts forever. Again, generally, that's a good precept, but there are exceptions for there are things that are eternal. One of those eternal things is the Everlasting Covenant.

The Everlasting Covenant was first spoken of in Genesis. God established the Everlasting Covenant with Abraham. However, the Covenant was not unto Abraham alone, but it was to Abraham's descendants. In this Covenant, God promised to always be their God, and the land we now call Israel would always belong to Abraham's descendants. The word "Everlasting" means it will last forever. In other words, it's Eternal.

> Genesis 17:7 And I will establish my covenant between me and thee and thy seed after thee in their generations **for an everlasting covenant**, to be a God unto thee, and to thy seed after thee.

God made another Covenant with Moses and the children of Israel who followed Moses out of Egypt. However, this Covenant was Not an Everlasting Covenant. In this Covenant, God promised to bless Israel in the Promised Land if they followed His Law. God knew from the beginning that they would fail. God told Moses that some while after Moses died, Israel would forsake the Lord and break the Covenant.

> Deuteronomy 31:16 And the LORD said unto Moses, Behold, thou shalt sleep with thy fathers; and this people will rise up, and go a whoring after the gods of the strangers of the land, whither they go to be among them, **and will forsake me, and break my covenant** which I have made with them.

Then, God tells Moses that after Israel has forsaken Him and broken the Covenant, He will forsake them.

> Deuteronomy 31:17 Then my anger shall be kindled against them in that day, **and I will forsake them**, and I will hide my face from them, and they shall be devoured, and many evils and troubles shall befall them; so that they will say in that day, Are not these evils come upon us, because our God is not among us?

When you make an agreement or a Covenant with someone, terms must be laid out and agreed upon up-front. Let's say we make an agreement that I'll mow your yard for $50 and you sign a contract saying that I alone will mow your yard.

Now let's say I mow your yard and charge you $100. I tell you that I forgot to mention that I charge a $50 fuel surcharge on top of the $50 mowing fee. People do things just like this every day. Nevertheless, if I did that, I'd be breaking the contract because the contract we signed said nothing of a $50 fuel surcharge. When a Covenant is made between two parties, one party can't add to it without the other's consent.

Galatians 3:15 Brethren, I speak after the manner of men; Though it be but a man's covenant, **yet if it be confirmed, no man disannulleth, or addeth thereto.**

When God made the Everlasting Covenant with Abraham, there was no mention of him or his descendants having to keep the Law. The Everlasting Covenant was made with Abraham and his Seed. Paul tells us that the Seed God was referring to was Jesus Christ.

Galatians 3:16 Now **to Abraham and his seed were the promises made.** He saith not, And to seeds, as of many; but as of one, **And to thy seed, which is Christ.**

So, the Covenant that was made with Moses, which was according to the Law, could not void the Everlasting Covenant that was made between God and Abraham. The Law was given to Moses, not to Abraham.

Galatians 3:17 And this I say, **that the covenant, that was confirmed before of God in Christ, the law,** which was four hundred and thirty years after, **cannot disannul**, that it should make the promise of none effect.

When we Trust in Jesus and are Born Again, we become Children of God, and we become spiritual descendants of Abraham. In other words, we become part of the Everlasting Covenant that God made with Abraham!

> Galatians 3:26 For ye are all the children of God by faith in Christ Jesus.
> Galatians 3:29 And **if ye be Christ's, then are ye Abraham's seed, and heirs according to the promise**.

Just as God told Moses, Israel broke the Covenant. God put up with them for hundreds of years and gave them time to repent, but they kept falling into idol worship and following other gods. Eventually, God had enough and declared the Covenant was broken, and both Israel and Judah went into captivity. The Jews were conquered by Babylon during the days of the Prophet Jeremiah who warned them what was going to happen.

> Jeremiah 11:10 They are turned back to the iniquities of their forefathers, which refused to hear my words; and they went after other gods to serve them: **the house of Israel and the house of Judah have broken my covenant which I made with their fathers.**
>
> Jeremiah 11:11 Therefore thus saith the LORD, Behold, I will bring evil upon them, which they shall not be able to escape; and **though they shall cry unto me, I will not hearken unto them.**

Jeremiah is known as the "Weeping Prophet". Along with the book named after him, he also wrote "Lamentations" which means to grieve or weep. It was a very sad time in Israel during the days of his prophecy.

However, Jeremiah's message wasn't all doom and gloom. Jeremiah also prophesied of the New Covenant. God says this Covenant is not like the one that He made with Moses.

> Jeremiah 31:31 Behold, the days come, saith the LORD, that I will make **a new covenant** with the house of Israel, and with the house of Judah:
>
> Jeremiah 31:32 **Not according to the covenant that I made with their fathers** in the day that I took them by the hand to bring them out of the land of Egypt; which my covenant they brake, although I was an husband unto them, saith the LORD:

In the New Covenant, God puts His law into the hearts of His people. Also, everyone who is part of the New Covenant "Knows God and He Knows them". This means God has a personal relationship with them.

> Jeremiah 31:33 But this shall be the covenant that I will make with the house of Israel; After those days, saith the LORD, **I will put my law in their inward parts,** and write it in their hearts; and will be their God, and they shall be my people.
>
> Jeremiah 31:34 And they shall teach no more every man his neighbour, and every man his brother, saying, Know the LORD: for **they shall all know me, from the least of them unto the greatest of them,** saith the LORD: for I will forgive their iniquity, and I will remember their sin no more.

God also says this Covenant is an Everlasting Covenant. This means it will not be broken! It is Eternal!

> Jeremiah 32:40 And **I will make an everlasting covenant with them**, that I will not turn away from them, to do them good; but **I will put my fear in their hearts, that they shall not depart from me.**

Ezekial also prophesies of the Everlasting Covenant. God says through Ezekial that Israel broke the Covenant (the one given to Moses), but He then tells them that He is going to establish an Everlasting Covenant with them.

> Ezekiel 16:59 For thus saith the Lord GOD; I will even deal with thee as thou hast done, which hast despised the oath **in breaking the covenant.**
>
> Ezekiel 16:60 Nevertheless I will remember my covenant with thee in the days of thy youth, and **I will establish unto thee an everlasting covenant.**

God also says though Ezekial, that the Everlasting Covenant will be a Covenant of Peace.

> Ezekiel 37:26 Moreover I will make **a covenant of peace** with them; **it shall be an everlasting covenant** with them: and I will place them, and multiply them, and will set my sanctuary in the midst of them for evermore.

We are shown in Isaiah that this Covenant of Peace will not be removed. God promises that the mountain and hills will depart and be removed before His kindness is removed from those in this Covenant.

> Isaiah 54:10 For the mountains shall depart, and the hills be removed; but <u>my kindness shall not depart from thee</u>, **neither shall the covenant of my peace be removed**, saith the LORD that hath mercy on thee.

The Covenant promises Everlasting Kindness & Mercy from God.

| |
|---|
| Isaiah 54:8 In a little wrath I hid my face from thee for a moment; but **with everlasting kindness will I have mercy on thee**, saith the LORD thy Redeemer. |

Everyone in this Covenant is also personally taught or guided by the Lord.

| | |
|---|---|
| Isaiah 54:13 And **all thy children shall be taught of the LORD**; and great shall be the peace of thy children. | John 6:45 **It is written in the prophets, And they shall be all taught of God.** Every man therefore that hath heard, and hath learned of the Father, cometh unto me. |

You may say that God says the Everlasting Covenant is with Israel. Well, it is, but when we are Born Again through Faith in Jesus, we as Children of God are grafted into true Israel or as Paul says the "Israel of God". Ezekial also prophesied of the "strangers" receiving inheritance in the land. This was strictly forbidden in the Covenant with Moses. He also says that the "Stranger" would be just like the natural-born Israelite.

| |
|---|
| Ezekiel 47:22 And it shall come to pass, that ye shall divide it by lot for an inheritance unto you, and to **the strangers that sojourn among you**, which shall beget children among you: and **they shall be unto you as born in the country among the children of Israel**; <u>**they shall have inheritance with you among the tribes of Israel.**</u> |

This was a huge mystery and still is to the Jews because in their minds the land was only for the physical descendants of Jacob. God revealed this mystery to Paul and showed him that this is fulfilled in the Gentile members of Christ's Church.

> Ephesians 3:3 How that by revelation **he made known unto me the mystery**; (as I wrote afore in few words,
>
> Ephesians 3:6 **That the Gentiles should be fellowheirs**, and of the same body, **and partakers of his promise in Christ by the gospel:**

Paul also shows us that God's promises in the Everlasting Covenant, are according to Faith. Because of this, God's promises are Sure to the Believer. In other words, we don't have to hope that we are measuring up to the Law in order to receive our inheritance, but we can know that we are Children of God through Faith in Jesus. Also, Paul wants to make clear that we are also spiritual children of Abraham.

> Romans 4:13 For the promise, that he should be the heir of the world, was not to Abraham, or to his seed, through the law, **but through the righteousness of faith.**
>
> Romans 4:16 **Therefore it is of faith, that it might be by grace**; to the end the promise might be **sure to all the seed**; not to that only which is of the law, but to that also which is of **the faith of Abraham; who is the father of us all,**

The Covenant with Moses was dedicated by blood. An animal was killed, and its blood was sprinkled on the people. This was a picture of the New Covenant and the blood of Jesus being sprinkled on us. Shortly before Jesus went to the cross, He told us that His blood was the blood of the New Covenant.

Matthew 26:28 For **this is my blood of the new testament**, which is shed for many for the remission of sins.

God says in Zechariah that it's because of the Blood of Jesus that we are saved from Hell. Another word for Hell in the Bible is the Pit. We were prisoners of the Pit until we were rescued by the Blood of Jesus.

Zechariah 9:11 As for thee also, **by the blood of thy covenant** I have sent forth thy prisoners **out of the pit wherein is no water**.

And so the Lord who is our Great Shepherd, established the Everlasting Covenant through His blood.

Hebrews 13:20 Now the God of peace, that brought again from the dead <u>our Lord Jesus, that great shepherd of the sheep</u>, **through the blood of the everlasting covenant,**

Promises of the Everlasting Covenant:

It is an Everlasting/Eternal Covenant.
It is not in accordance with the Covenant of Moses.
God will put His Law in the hearts of the people.
He will be their God and they will be His people.
Everyone in the Covenant will Know God and He will Know them.
God will forgive their iniquity and remember their sins no more.
God will put His fear in the hearts of the people so they will not depart from Him.
God will give the people Peace, Kindness, and Mercy and promises that none of which will be removed.
God will personally teach and guide all the people.
God promises His Spirit and the testimony of the people will not depart from them.

If you've been Born Again and are in the Everlasting Covenant with God, everything that happens to you will in some way work for your good. But what if it's bad or involves sin you say? In one way or another God will make it benefit you in the long run through teaching and chastisement. Before you think that's an excuse to sin, realize that God is interested more in your spiritual benefit than a physical one. Also, God is more interested in eternity than this physical world that's going to be destroyed.

Romans 8:28 And we know that **all things work together for good to them that love God, to them who are the called** according to his purpose.

You see, if you're Born Again, God foreknew (knew ahead of time) you would believe before you ever believed, and He's been using everything that happens in your life to make you more like Jesus.

Romans 8:29 For **whom he did foreknow, he also did predestinate to be conformed to the image of his Son**, that he might be the firstborn among many brethren.

Moreover, if God foreknew you and predestinated (pre-determined) to make you more like Jesus, He Called you to Himself, He Justified you, and He's going to Glorify you. This is an unbroken chain. All those who He foreknew would believe will be glorified!

Romans 8:30 Moreover whom he did predestinate, them he also called: and whom he called, them he also justified: and whom he justified, **them he also glorified**.

If God died for us when we were sinners and His enemies to save us, how much more will He not use His power to keep us saved?

Romans 5:8 But God commendeth his love toward us, in that, while we were yet sinners, Christ died for us.
Romans 5:9 **Much more then, being now justified by his blood, we shall be saved from wrath through him**.
Romans 5:10 For if, when we were enemies, we were reconciled to God by the death of his Son, **much more, being reconciled, we shall be saved by his life.**

Paul understood the promises of the Everlasting Covenant. It's because of these promises that we can be sure that our Salvation is secure. If someone thinks a truly Born-Again person can lose their Salvation, they need to think about how they would lose it. Will they lose it because they fail to keep the Law? That won't work because keeping the Law is not part of this Covenant. What if they leave Christ? Well, God has promised to keep us from doing that, so if you leave Christ, you were never a part of the Covenant to begin with. We stay saved the same way we got saved which is Trusting in the Blood of Jesus and God has promised to keep us in His love. Because of God's promises, Paul understood that nothing can separate us from God's love.

Romans 8:31 What shall we then say to these things? **If God be for us, who can be against us?**

Romans 8:32 He that spared not his own Son, but delivered him up for us all, how shall he not with him also freely give us all things?

Romans 8:33 Who shall lay any thing to the charge of God's elect? **It is God that justifieth.**

Romans 8:**38 For I am persuaded, that neither death, nor life, nor angels, nor principalities, nor powers, nor things present, nor things to come,**

Romans 8:**39 Nor height, nor depth, nor any other creature, shall be able to separate us from the love of God, which is in Christ Jesus our Lord.**

A list of things that are unable to separate Believers from God's Love:

Death:  When you die, you won't be separated from God

Life:    Nothing in your life will separate you from God

Angels:  No Angel can separate you from God, this includes Satan

Principalities:  No prince, chief, king, president (includes angelic rulers)

Powers:  No demonic power or witchcraft, or earthy power

Things Present:  Nothing happening in your present life

Things to Come:  Nothing that will happen to you in the future

Height: Nothing in Heaven above will separate you from God's love

Depth:  Nothing in Hell can separate you from God's love

No other Creature:  Anything you can imagine that wasn't mentioned prior can separate you from God's love


Remember, saved people have always been saved by Faith.  God told Moses that the people would forsake Him and break the Covenant, after which He would forsake them.  However, God had a different message for Joshua.  God knew that Joshua was a true Believer and so God told Moses to tell Joshua that He would never fail or forsake him.  God also spoke this to Joshua directly.

| Deuteronomy 31:6 Be strong and of a good courage, fear not, nor be afraid of them: for the LORD thy God, he it is that doth go with thee; **he will not fail thee, nor forsake thee.** | Joshua 1:5 There shall not any man be able to stand before thee all the days of thy life: as I was with Moses, so I will be with thee: **I will not fail thee, nor forsake thee.** |

The word "Forsake" means to totally turn away from something and to abandon it. God promises that when a person is Saved through Faith, He will never Forsake them. Another promise of the Everlasting Covenant is that God will Never Forsake us.

> Hebrews 13:5 Let your conversation be without covetousness; and be content with such things as ye have: for he hath said, **I will never leave thee, nor forsake thee.**

Now, I have a Secret to tell you. It's not actually my Secret. God had a Secret that was only revealed to certain people. This Secret started in the Garden of Eden. When a person feared God and was willing to trust in Him, He gave them a Secret Message. He gave this Message to Adam, Enoch, Noah, Abraham, Job, Moses, Ruth, David, Esther, and many more. This Message was the Secret to Salvation. It was the Message of a Covenant.

> Psalm 25:14 The **secret of the LORD** is with them that fear him; and **he will shew them his covenant**.

The Message that was given to them was the Gospel of Christ. He told them that Salvation was by Grace through Faith in Christ. Christ hadn't yet come, but they were looking for Him and waiting for Him. Everyone who has ever found Salvation has found it the exact same way. There will be no one in Heaven who will be there because they followed the Law. Everyone you'll meet in Heaven will have the same Testimony. They will tell you how they were sinners who deserved Hell but were Saved by the Blood of Jesus.

Throughout time, God gave further revelation regarding the Covenant. They knew the Redeemer was coming but they didn't know when or how. So, God told Abraham that Christ would come from his descendants. Then, it was revealed Christ would come through Isaac, then Jacob, then Judah, and then David. Finally, when the time was right Jesus was born into the world and died for us all. At this point, God's Secret which He had kept since the beginning of the world was revealed.

> Romans 16:25 Now to him that is of power to stablish you according to my gospel, and the preaching of Jesus Christ, according to the revelation of the mystery, **which was kept secret since the world began,**

Sin can take the joy of our Salvation away at times. David lost his joy for a short time, but he never lost his salvation.

> Psalm 51:11 Cast me not away from thy presence; and take not thy holy spirit from me.
> Psalm 51:12 **Restore unto me the joy of thy salvation**; and uphold me with thy free spirit.

Although David felt like the Lord should, He never took His Spirit away from David. If you've been Born Again, God will never take His Spirit away from you either.

> 1 Samuel 16:13 Then Samuel took the horn of oil, and anointed him in the midst of his brethren: and **the Spirit of the LORD came upon David from that day forward.** So Samuel rose up, and went to Ramah.

David was a model of what a modern-day Christian is. David Trusted in the Lord with all his heart. When David sinned, God showed him mercy in ways that He hadn't shown mercy to other people. God made an Everlasting Covenant with David. As Christians, God has made an Everlasting Covenant with us as well. David said that this Covenant is all his Salvation. David also said the Covenant is Sure.

> 2 Samuel 23:5 Although my house be not so with God; yet **he hath made with me an everlasting covenant**, ordered in all things, **and sure: for this is all my salvation**, and all my desire, although he make it not to grow.

Like David, the Everlasting Covenant is all our Salvation as well. If you're a part of this Covenant you have EVERYTHING! If you're a part of this Covenant, your Salvation is Sure and Certain! The Eternal Security of the Believer is a Biblical Fact. We are Saved by the Lord and His Blood. We are kept Saved by the Lord and His Blood. He has promised that He's going to see our Salvation through to the end and take us Home. This is the Everlasting Covenant and the Sure Mercies of David.

> Isaiah 55:3 Incline your ear, and come unto me: hear, and your soul shall live; and **I will make an everlasting covenant with you, even the sure mercies of David.**